MW00990435

The
Mystery
Of Creation

WATCHMAN NEE

Translated from the Chinese

Christian Fellowship Publishers, Inc.
New York

ISBN 0–935008–52–7

Available from the Publishers at:

11515 Allecingie Parkway
Richmond, Virginia 23235

PRINTED IN U.S.A.

TRANSLATOR'S PREFACE

Man always wonders about himself as well as the things that surround him. He has tried for centuries to unlock the mystery of creation by observation and speculation. Yet the true story of creation would never have been told had not God revealed it to Moses. The challenge of God to human inquiry and research is the same today as it was in the days of Job: "Who is this that darkeneth counsel by words without knowledge? Gird up now thy loins like a man; for I will demand of thee, and declare thou unto me. Where wast thou when I laid the foundations of the earth? Declare, if thou hast understanding. Who determined the measures thereof, if thou knowest? Or who stretched the line upon it? Whereupon were the foundations thereof fastened? Or who laid the corner-stone thereof, when the morning stars sang together, and all the sons of God shouted for joy?" (Job. 38.2-7)

In this volume, Watchman Nee presents to us a Biblical interpretation of creation to which science attests. This is not meant to prove, however, that the story of creation as revealed in the Bible is scientifically true but to show instead that God is greater than science. Whereas God's word is forever true, the discipline of science must constantly be revised. How inexhaustible is God's revelation, that in giving the history of creation (as found in the letter of His word) He has also disclosed His principles of working in the

New as in the Old Creation. Hence an analogy of creation and Christian experience, an analysis of creation and the acts of Christ, and an anatomy of creation and dispensation are additionally presented in order to lead us into the spirit of God's word.

May we bow in wonder at "the depth of the riches both of the wisdom and the knowledge of God!" (Rom. 11.33)

CONTENTS

Being a series of messages written in Chinese by the author originally entitled "Meditations on Genesis," for publication in *Christian* Magazine from 1925 to 1927.

Scripture quotations are from the
American Standard Version of the Bible
(1901), unless otherwise indicated.

1 | Genesis and Geology

We believe the Bible is the word of God: every word is God-breathed. It is a constant weight in the minds of the godly that people should despise and even oppose God's word. The hearts of God's children are grieved because people do not respect God's statutes. And of the sixty-six books of the Bible, Genesis is subjected to more doubt and attacks than is any other. Those who oppose the Holy Bible frequently try to use geological periods and prehistorical fossils to overturn the clear revelation of God's word. According to these geological evidences, the earth has been in existence for tens of thousands of years. And hence to them the record of six thousand years of history in the Bible is untrustworthy. They accordingly wave the flag of science in their attack on the record of Genesis.

Many dear brethren in the Lord are really tossed by such storms of controversy due to their lack of learning. Although geology is not the basis for our meditation today, we would deal with it at the outset of our meditation on Genesis for the sake of the benefit of those brethren. By the grace of God we will together look into the word of God to discover how perfect is His word so that we may remain in His presence beholding His glory.

Let us understand, first of all, that Genesis is God's revelation; geology, on the other hand, is man's invention. Since God knows all the facts, His revelation can never be in error. Men can only see partially, hence their deduction is hardly accurate. If both Genesis and geology are before us, what we follow must be Genesis and not geology because God is behind Genesis. If Genesis and geology differ, the error must be on the side of geology, for the authority of the Bible is beyond questioning. Thank God our Father for giving us a perfect revelation. If there is any disagreement between God and men, we would rather forsake men and follow God. But if there is no difference between the word of God and that of men, will that not strengthen the faith of the weak to believe in the revelation which comes from heaven?

People often laugh at the creation story myths circulated among the Chinese, the Babylonians, and other ancient peoples. No scientist bothers to refute these mythic accounts. And why? Because these traditions have no intrinsic value; therefore, they are not worth any special attention. People's attitude towards the Bible, however, is quite different. Their very effort to resist the Scriptures proves the power of the Bible. The fact that they do not treat this Book the same as they treat the traditions of the nations demonstrates the ascendant position the Bible holds.

Who can read the first chapter of Genesis without being impressed by its uniqueness? Rather common, yet so marvelous! The facts are presented in such a straightforward manner that there is not a trace of theorizing. There is no attempt to argue and to prove the authenticity of the facts presented. The Author is not bound by the book since He is so much bigger than that about which He writes. He far transcends the universe simply because He is God. Now had the author been Moses—who would doubtless have written out of his own learning and wisdom—his writing would naturally have been influenced by Egyptian creation myths, for he was instructed in all the wisdom of that ancient people. But no one can ever discover in the Genesis account any trace of the Egyptian myth! And why? Because it was *God* who inspired Moses to write. If this were not so, how could Moses have possibly known that the earth originally came out of water?—a fact recognized in geology but only discovered in modern times. How can it be explained otherwise, if Moses had not received revelation? And as to the origin of life on earth, even though the Bible opposes the theory of evolution it does not reject the concept of progression: first the scaly fishes of the water and finally human beings on earth. Should not the scientists marvel at the record of Moses? Because the omniscient God revealed these facts, the one who received such revelation from Him cannot be in error.

Even so, the Bible is not a book of science. Its primary aim is rather to point sinners to Christ Jesus that they may receive the wisdom of salvation. Yet interestingly enough it contains no scientific error even though it basically is not a book on science. If there is any discrepancy between it and science, such discrepancy will be either due to man's misinterpretation of the Bible or to an inaccuracy in the conclusions of science. How many of the sure pronouncements of former geologists have over the years changed! What they affirmed in the past have been proven later to be mistakes. One observer, Cummings by name, has said that ''geology has made mistakes, and it will make mistakes again. Those hurriedly announced loud proclamations may prove to be inaccurate in the future.'' Since the Bible was never intended to teach people science, it simply narrates the ''fact'' of creation without explaining ''why.'' Scientists like to explain the ''why'' (and without a doubt they have succeeded much in doing so), but they should not proceed to overturn fact by their reasonings which are based on limited observations. For God knows everything, and what He says is fact. How can men in their searching to know the why of something deny the authority of God and trust in their own opinions? It is good to have knowledge, but there is a foolishness which is more blessed.

The general concept among Christians regarding the first chapter of Genesis is that the very first verse is a kind of general introduction or premise, and that the works which are done in the six days to follow explain it. In other words, they take the words ''In the beginning God created the heavens and the earth'' as the subject of Chapter 1. The writer of Genesis, so they speculate, outlines what he intends to say in the first sentence and then proceeds to explain it in detail. Having mentioned when God created the heavens and the earth, he then continues by telling what condition the earth is in and how God day after day creates light, air, earth, plants, animals, and so forth. Such is the popular view as to how Genesis 1 narrates the creation story and how the universe was created out of waste and void. Yet those who study carefully the first chapter of sacred Scripture deem this interpretation to be erroneous. Due to this erroneous interpretation and not due to the Bible's narration itself, a great controversy has arisen between the church and the world. Many young people, for example, doubt the accuracy of the Bible when they learn of such ''discrepancy'' in the face of particular geological evidences.

In the original Hebrew, this initial verse of the first chapter of Genesis contains seven words which carry within themselves a sense of independence. These divinely revealed words do not say that in the beginning God ''formed'' or ''made'' the world out of certain raw materials. No, the heavens and the earth were *created*. This word ''created'' is ''bara'' in the original. So that in the beginning God *bara* the heavens and the earth. This word ''bara'' is used three more times in Genesis 1 and 2: (1st) ''And God created [bara] the great sea-monsters, and every living creature that moveth, wherewith the waters swarmed, after their kind, and every winged bird after its kind''

(1.21); (2nd) "And God created [bara] man in his own image, in the image of God created he him; male and female created he them" (1.27); and (3rd) "And God blessed the seventh day, and hallowed it; because that in it he rested from all his work which God had created [bara] and made" (2.3). To "create" is to "call the things that are not, as though they were" (Rom. 4.17). These sea-monsters and living things not only had physical bodies but also had an animated life within them. They therefore required a direct creative act of God. Thus it is only reasonable that the Scriptures should use the word "created" rather than the word "made" in these passages. In similar manner, though man's body was formed out of the dust of the ground, his soul and spirit could not be made out of any physical material, and hence the Bible declared that "God created man in his own image."

In the first two chapters of Genesis three different words are used for the act of creation: (1) "bara"—calling into being without the aid of pre-existing material. This we have already touched upon; (2) "asah" —which is quite different from "bara," since the latter denotes the idea of creating without any material whereas "asah" signifies the making, fashioning, or preparing out of existing material. For instance, a carpenter can *make* a chair, but he cannot *create* one. The works of the Six Days in Genesis are mainly of the order of "asah"; (3) "yatsar"—which means to shape or mold as a potter does with clay. This word is used in Genesis 2.7 as follows: "And Jehovah God formed man of the dust of the ground." Interestingly, Isaiah 43.7 illustrates the meaning and connection of all three of these words: "every one that is called by my name, and whom I have *created* for my glory, whom I have *formed*, yea, whom I have *made.*" "Created" signifies a calling into being out of nothing; "formed" denotes a fashioning into appointed form; and "made" means a preparing out of pre-existing material.

The words "In the beginning" reinforce the thought of God creating the heavens and the earth out of nothing. There is really no need to theorize; since God has so spoken, let men simply believe. How absurd for finite minds to search out the works of God which He performed at the beginning! "By faith we *understand* that the worlds have been framed by the word of God" (Heb. 11.3). Who can answer God's challenge to Job concerning creation (see Job 38)?

"In the beginning God created the heavens and the earth." This heaven is not the firmament immediately surrounding the earth; rather, it points to the heaven where the stars are. It has not undergone any change since it was created, but the earth is no longer the same.

To understand the first chapter of Genesis, it is of utmost importance that we distinguish the "earth" mentioned in verse 1 from the "earth" spoken of in verse 2. For the condition of the earth referred to in verse 2 is not what God had created originally. Now we know that "God is not a God of confusion" (1 Cor. 14.33). And hence when it states that in the beginning God created the earth, what He created was therefore perfect. So that the waste and void of the earth spoken of in verse 2 was not the original condition of the earth as God first created it. Would God ever create an earth whose primeval condition would be waste and void? A true understanding of this verse will solve the apparent problem.

"Thus saith Jehovah that created the heavens, the God that formed the earth and made it, that established it and created it not a waste, that formed it to be inhabited: I am Jehovah; and there is none else" (Is. 45.18). How clear God's word is. The word "waste" here is "tohu" in Hebrew, which signifies "desolation" or "that which is desolate." It says here that the earth which God created was not a waste. Why then does Genesis 1.2 state that "the earth was waste"? This may be easily resolved. In the beginning God created the heavens and the earth (Gen. 1.1). At that time, the earth which God had created was *not* a waste; but *later on,* in passing through a great catastrophe, the earth *did* become waste and void. So that all which is mentioned from verse 3 onward does not refer to the original creation but to *the restoration of the earth.* God created the heavens and the earth in the beginning; but He subsequently used the Six Days to remake the earth habitable. Genesis 1.1 was the original world; Genesis 1.3 onward is our present world; while Genesis 1.2 describes the desolate condition which was the earth's during the transitional period following its original creation and before our present world.

Such an interpretation cannot only be arrived at on the basis of Isaiah 45.18, it can also be supported on the basis of other evidences. The conjunctive word "and" in verse 2 can also be translated as "but": "In the beginning God created the heavens and the earth, *but* the earth was waste and void." G. H. Pember, in his book *Earth's Earliest Ages,* wrote that

> the "and" according to Hebrew usage—as well as that of most other languages—proves that the first verse is not a compendium of what follows, but a statement of the first event in the record. For if it were a mere summary, the second verse would be the actual commencement of the history, and certainly would not begin with a copulative. A good illustration of this may be found in the fifth chapter of Genesis (Gen. 5.1). There the opening words, "This is the book of the generations of Adam," are a compendium of the chapter, and, consequently, the next sentence begins without a copulative. We have, therefore, in the second verse of Genesis no first detail of a general statement in the preceding sentence, but the record of an altogether distinct and subsequent event, which did not affect the sidereal [starry] heaven, but only the earth and its immediate surroundings. And what that event was we must now endeavour to discover.*

Over a hundred years ago, Dr. Chalmers pointed out that the words "the earth *was* waste" might equally be translated "the earth *became* waste." Dr. I. M. Haldeman, G. H. Pember, and others showed

---

*G. H. Pember, *Earth's Earliest Ages,* New Edition, edited with additions by G. H. Lang (Grand Rapids: Kregel Publications, 1975), p. 31. (The original work of Pember, under the same title, was initially published in 1876 by Hodder and Stoughton. Later editions were issued by Pickering and Inglis and the Fleming H. Revell Co.)

that the Hebrew word for "was" here has been translated "became" in Genesis 19.26: "His wife looked back from behind him, and she *became* a pillar of salt." If this same Hebrew word can be translated in 19.26 as "became," why can it not be translated as "became" in 1.2? Furthermore, the word "became" in 2.7 ("and man became a living soul") is the same word as is found in Genesis 1.2. So that it is not at all arbitrary for anyone to translate "was" as "became" here: "In the beginning God created the heavens and the earth, [but] the earth *became* waste and void." The earth which God created originally was not waste, it only later became waste.

"In the beginning God *created* the heavens and the earth" (Gen. 1.1) and "in six days Jehovah *made* heaven and earth, the sea, and all that in them is" (Ex. 20.11). Comparing these two verses, we can readily see that the world in Genesis 1.1 was quite different from the world that came after Genesis 1.3. In the *beginning*, God *created* the heavens and the earth. In the *Six Days* God *made* the heaven and earth and sea. Who can measure the distance that exists between "created" and "made"? The one is a calling into being things out of nothing, the other is a working on something already there. Man can make but cannot create; God can create as well as make. Hence Genesis records that in the beginning God created the heavens and the earth, but later on the earth had become waste and void due to a tremendous catastrophe, after which God commenced to remake the heaven, earth and sea and all the creatures in them. 2 Peter 3.5–7 expresses the same thought as well: the heavens and the earth in verse 5 are the original heavens and earth referred to in Genesis 1.1; the earth mentioned in verse 6 that was overflowed with water and which perished is the earth covered with water which became waste and void as mentioned in Genesis 1.2; and the heavens and the earth that now are as spoken of in verse 7 are the restored heavens and earth after Genesis 1.3. Hence the works of God during the Six Days are quite different from His creative work done in the beginning.

The more we study Genesis 1, the more we are convinced that the above is the true interpretation. In the first day, God commanded light to shine forth. Before this first day, the earth had already been existing, but it was now buried in water, dwelt in darkness, and was waste and void. On the third day, God did not create the earth. He merely commanded it to come out of water. F. W. Grant has stated that "the six days' work merely sets the earth into a new program; it does not create it out of nothing."* On the first day, God did not *create* light, He instead commanded light to shine out of darkness. The light was already there. Neither did God create heaven on the second day. The heaven here is not the starry heaven but the atmospheric heaven, that which surrounds the earth. Where, then, did all these come from if they were not created during the Six Days? The one answer is that they were created at the time of the first verse of Genesis 1. So that subsequently, there was no need to create but simply to remake.

---

*A free translation.—*Translator*

"In the beginning God created the heavens and the earth." Note that there is no detailed description here. We therefore do not know whether the original heaven and earth were created instantaneously or through many ages. Was it done in thousands of years or in millions of years? In what shape and how large? We only know that God created the heavens and the earth in the beginning. Neither do we know how many years elapsed between the time of the first verse and that of the second verse of Genesis 1. We do not know when God created the heavens and the earth, nor do we know how long was the period after the original creation that the desolation described in verse 2 occurred. But we do believe that the original, perfect creation must have passed through many many years before it became waste and void. Such a long period would be enough to cover the so-called pre-historic age. All the years which geology demands and all the so-called geologic periods which it distributes among those years can fall into this time frame. We do not know how long the earth underwent change nor how many changes there were before it became waste and void because the Scriptures do not tell us these things. Yet we *can* affirm that the Bible never states that *the age of the earth* is but six thousand years in length. It merely shows that the *history of man* is approximately six thousand years old. By understanding the first two verses of Scripture, we can recognize that there is no contradiction between the Bible and geology. The attack of geologists against the Bible is merely beating the air. How marvelous is the word of God.

We do not present this interpretation in order to pacify science. For the revelation of God never yields to man's reasoning. We will not forsake the authority of God's word in order to make compromise with the conclusions of men. Nor do we intend to attempt to reconcile science with the Bible (for contradiction is to be expected since "the mind of the flesh is enmity against God"—Rom. 8.7). For such an interpretation as we have presented here was put forward even in the early church, long before geology had become a discipline of science.

What a Christian believes is not the wisdom of men but the word of God. Aside from the rock of the Bible, we need no other ground on which to stand. As long as the Scriptures declare it, that is deemed final to us. How lamentable it is that many so-called defenders of the faith too readily give ground and alter the Scriptures so as to reconcile them with human theories. An example of this is given by A. W. Pink, who noted that after the translation of a certain Assyrian tablet, people such as mentioned above enthusiastically reported that the Old Testament history was now being verified by that tablet. This is really turning things upside down. Does the word of God need any verification? Let us clearly understand that if the record on the Assyrian tablet coincides with that of the Bible, it only shows that the tablet has no historical error. And if they do not agree, it merely proves that the tablet is erroneous. In a similar way, if the teaching of science agrees with the Bible, the latter verifies the truth of science. But in case they do not agree, the Scriptures attest to the falsehood of science's hypothesis. Natural man will of course laugh at our logic, yet this scornful attitude in itself ironically substantiates what the word of God declares when it states that "the natural man receiveth not the things of the Spirit of God: for they are foolishness unto him; and he cannot know them, because they are spiritually judged" (1 Cor. 2.14)! Let us therefore not compromise our dignity in order to agree with the world. Let us not alter the Bible to suit the taste of men.

How marvelous is the first chapter of Genesis! One verse is used to proclaim the original creation, a single verse is called upon to pronounce the ruin of the world, and less than thirty verses are utilized to promulgate the remaking of the world! Who else in the universe could write a chapter comparable to Genesis 1? So difficult a topic, yet so clearly stated. So long a history, but so simply put. It is plainly not science, and yet it is scientifically accurate. If it was not written by God, then who was it who could write such a chapter? The reason why God does not say more is because He will reveal to men only that which pertains to men's relationship with Him. As one Biblical scholar has observed:

> This revelation from God is not a history by Him of all that He has done, but what has been given to man for his profit, the truth as to what he has to say to. Its object is to communicate to man all that regards his own relationship with God. . . . But historically the revelation is partial. It communicates what is for the conscience and spiritual affections of man. . . . Thus no mention is made of any heavenly beings. . . . Thus also, as regards this

earth, except the fact of its creation, nothing is said of it beyond what relates to the present form of it.*

Indeed, what God has revealed is not for the sake of gratifying the curiosity of men, but for the purpose of expressing His divine character, the sinful nature of man, the way of salvation, and the future glory and punishment. How dangerous is worldly knowledge, for men out of their self-conceit will attack God with their limited knowledge.

How difficult for the intellectual man to be humble! Men always seek after knowledge, but God is unwilling to enhance such pursuit with His revelation. Consequently, He says very little here about creation. What we now need is not more science but deeper spirituality which will last on into eternity. Let us praise God our Father for He is so merciful. He not only created us but also remakes us, that we may be a new creation in Christ. How sweet is the name of the Lord Jesus! What grace it is that God has given His Son to us!

---

*J. N. Darby, *Synopsis of the Books of the Bible* (Kingston-on-Thames: Stow Hill Bible and Truth Depot, 1948), I:7–8.

2 | The Original World and the Cause of Its Desolation

We have already seen how in the beginning God created a perfect heaven and earth. Later on—we do not know how long afterwards—the original beautiful earth became waste and void. However, God rose up and remade this world. In six days, He restored this desolate world. We will deal with the works of these Six Days in a later chapter, but here we would inquire as to why this original world was turned into waste. Why did God allow the work of His hand to be destroyed? For what reason did such a terrifying catastrophe fall upon such a beautiful earth?

The subject we will examine is not explicitly stated in the Scriptures, but it is found implicitly in many passages. By these intimations of light we may understand a little more concerning the original world and the cause of its desolation. Only the word of God can guide our thought. As a matter of fact, the understanding of His word will edify us with regard to whatever subject we may take up. The vanity of vanities is to rely on man's mental supposition instead of holding on to the word of God.

Now as we look into Genesis chapter 3 (and even though Satan is nowhere named there), we can know for a certainty that the serpent mentioned therein was indeed Satan's instrument; in fact, it was probably Satan himself in disguise. For it is said in Revelation 12.9 that "the great dragon was cast down, the old serpent, he that is called the Devil and Satan, the deceiver of the whole world." Since Genesis 1 does not record the creation of Satan, it can legitimately be asked: Where did *he* come from? Furthermore, we see mention made throughout the Old Testament of many evil spirits; throughout the Gospels as well we encounter many of them quite frequently. Where did *they* come from? Moreover, we do not learn of the creation of angels, even though these angels are often mentioned throughout the Bible. Where also did *they* come from? All these questions are legitimately related to our problem. Now inasmuch as nothing was mentioned during the work of the Six Days in Genesis about the creation of angels or other supernatural beings, we must assume that they could not have been created at that time. If they were not created during the Six Days' period, when *were* they created? The only possible answer is that they were the creatures of the former, original world. In this connection, we ought to consider the observations of G. H. Pember:

> As the fossil remains clearly show, not only were disease and death—inseparable companions of sin—then prevalent among the living creatures of

the earth, but even ferocity and slaughter. And the fact proves that these remains have nothing to do with our world; since the Bible declares that all things made by God during the six days were very good, and that no evil was in them till Adam sinned. . . . Since, then, the fossil remains are those of creatures anterior to Adam, and yet show evident tokens of disease, death, and mutual destruction, they must have belonged to another world and have a sin-stained history of their own, a history which ended in the ruin of themselves and their habitation.*

By reading Jeremiah 4.23–26 we may know why the earth became waste and void: "broken down at the presence of Jehovah, and before his fierce anger" (v.26). Why was the Lord angry? Most likely it was due to the sin of the creatures at that time. Isaiah 24.1 sheds further light: "Behold, Jehovah maketh the earth empty, and maketh it waste." What made Him willing to destroy the earth which He had originally created? By looking at the history of our own world, we may deduce that it was also because of the sin of those creatures who inhabited the original earth. Accordingly, God could not but judge them.

Ezekiel 28 and The Origin of Satan

Though in studying Genesis we do not learn the origin of Satan, nevertheless, as we probe into the cause for the desolation of the earth in the beginning we naturally can conclude that this must be due to the

---

*G. H. Pember, *op. cit.,* pp. 34–35.

enemy. Apart from Satan there can be found no other reason in the Bible to account for this catastrophe.

Let us now examine another passage in the Scriptures which seems to tell us the origin of this adversary of God whom we shall discover to be the cause for the desolation of the original world. It is Ezekiel 28.1–19. These nineteen verses can be divided into two parts: the first from verses 1 to 10 is the prophet's warning to the Prince of Tyre; the second part from verses 11 to 19 is the prophet's lamentation for the King of Tyre. The first part regarding the Prince of Tyre is easily understood. He was proud and arrogant, who considered himself to be god and wiser than Daniel. His heart was lifted up because of his riches gained through trafficking in commerce. Therefore God punished him and destroyed him by the hands of the terror of the nations. For not long after this prophecy was spoken, Nebuchadnezzar, King of the Chaldeans, came and destroyed Tyre. The Jewish historian Josephus thought this prince of Tyre was Ittobalus, whereas in Phoenician history he was called Ittobaal II. We today know that this prophecy has already been fulfilled. Hence we encounter no difficulty in explaining verses 1 to 10. But as we read on from verse 11 we find many places hard to understand. Since this is closely related to what we are examining, we will quote this second part in full:

> Moreover the word of Jehovah came unto me, saying, Son of man, take up a lamentation over the king of Tyre, and say unto him, Thus saith the Lord Jehovah: Thou sealest up the sum, full of

wisdom, and perfect in beauty. Thou wast in Eden, the garden of God; every precious stone was thy covering, the sardius, the topaz, and the diamond, the beryl, the onyx, and the jasper, the sapphire, the emerald, and the carbuncle, and gold: the workmanship of thy tabrets and of thy pipes was in thee; in the day that thou wast created they were prepared. Thou wast the anointed cherub that covereth: and I set thee, so that thou wast upon the holy mountain of God; thou hast walked up and down in the midst of the stones of fire. Thou wast perfect in thy ways from the day that thou wast created, till unrighteousness was found in thee. By the abundance of thy traffic they filled the midst of thee with violence, and thou hast sinned: therefore have I cast thee as profane out of the mountain of God; and I have destroyed thee, O covering cherub, from the midst of the stones of fire. Thy heart was lifted up because of thy beauty; thou hast corrupted thy wisdom by reason of thy brightness: I have cast thee to the ground; I have laid thee before kings, that they may behold thee. By the multitude of thine iniquities, in the unrighteousness of thy traffic, thou hast profaned thy sanctuaries; therefore have I brought forth a fire from the midst of thee; it hath devoured thee, and I have turned thee to ashes upon the earth in the sight of all them that behold thee. All they that know thee among the peoples shall be astonished at thee: thou art become a terror, and thou shalt nevermore have any being. (28.11–19)

This lengthy passage is truly difficult to understand because there are many words here which cannot be applied to human beings. If the King of Tyre is but a human being, how can you explain the things mentioned from verses 11 to 15? When was the King of Tyre ever in the Garden of Eden, in the holy mountain of God? How could he in the least be the cherub who covered the ark? Nothing mentioned here was ever the experience of the King of Tyre. Yet neither can we spiritualize everything whenever we encounter difficulty.

I consider the first part (verses 1-10) which is addressed to the Prince of Tyre as being applicable to Ittobalus but that the second part (verses 11-19)—which is a lamentation against the King of Tyre—points to the future Antichrist. Verse 2 mentions Tyre as being in the midst of the sea. In reading Daniel 11.41-45 we know that when the future Antichrist will be in Palestine he will most probably stay in Tyre. Hence he is called the King of Tyre. Actually the Antichrist is but Satan incarnated. So that many of the things here have reference to Satan himself. In the opinion of J. N. Darby, "Verses 11-19, while continuing to speak of Tyre, go, I think, much farther, and disclose, though darkly, the fall and the ways of Satan, become through our sin the prince and god of this world."* Arno C. Gaebelein feels the same way: "The King of Tyre is a type of the last man of sin (the Antichrist). Behind this wicked King we see another power—which is Satan. For at that time Satan was the power behind the King of Tyre; now he still is the god of this world who controls the nations."**

If we study the Bible carefully, we will see that it is not against the normal teaching of God's word to join

---

*J. N. Darby, *op. cit.*, II:294.
**A free translation.—*Translator*

Satan and the Antichrist together. We know, in spite of the fact people have their own will, that their movement is either the result of the working of God in them (Phil. 2.13) or the result of the working of the evil spirit (Eph. 2.2). Men do not have complete liberty. Ordinarily people of the world are under the control of the evil spirits. Sometimes, where mighty issues are at stake, Satan himself may step in and work. We saw how he came personally to tempt Christ in the wilderness; how later on he used Peter to dissuade Christ from the cross; and finally how he entered Judas' heart in order to destroy Christ. In the last days he will join with the Antichrist in the arena of the world. Hence the Bible states this: "Even he [the lawless one], whose coming is according to the working of Satan" (2 Thess. 2.9). For Satan shall give him "his power, and his throne, and great authority" (Rev. 13.2). In view of the fact that Antichrist is Satan incarnated, the Holy Spirit speaks of them as one. So that in these verses all the supernatural things have reference to Satan himself while the rest speaks of the Antichrist. Now our purpose here is not to engage in research on the Antichrist but to know the creatures of the original world and to discover the reason for its desolation. Consequently, we shall set aside the places where Antichrist is referred to and focus our attention on those things involving Satan.

"How art thou fallen from heaven, O day-star, son of the morning!" (Is. 14.12) Before the archangel's fall, he was called the Day-Star, the Son of the Morning. After his rebellion, however, he is called Satan—which means the adversary.

"Thou sealest up the sum, full of wisdom, and perfect in beauty" (Ez. 28.12). This was the archangel's condition prior to his sin. He was higher than all the other angels. These terms—"the sum . . . full . . . perfect"—indicate that he was the greatest among the original creatures. God placed him above all others. Moreover, he was full of wisdom, indicative of his understanding of God's will. Probably he had at that time the office of a prophet.

"Thou wast in Eden, the garden of God; every precious stone was thy covering" (v.13a). In Genesis 3 we see the presence of Satan. He was there not having every precious stone as his covering but rather he was there as a tempter to Adam and Eve. And hence these two Edens do not co-exist. At the time of Adam's Eden, Satan had already fallen; but in the Eden mentioned here, Satan had not fallen yet. So that *this* garden of Eden must have existed *before* Adam's Eden. If so, it must have belonged to the former world, not to the present world. It can be likened to the New Jerusalem in the future, having many precious stones such as the sardis, jasper, and so forth. The Eden which Adam inhabited, though, was not so. The Bible draws attention only to the trees in it, nothing being said of its bejeweled covering. Hence the Eden here must be different from Adam's Eden. It was much earlier in time. The precious stones which the archangel wore remind us of the precious stones which Aaron the priest had on him (see Ex. 28). This therefore intimates that probably God had established him as a priest.

"The workmanship of thy tabrets and of thy pipes was in thee" (v.13b). In the Bible we find that musical instruments were used by kings. We notice, for example, how David played the harp before King Saul, how, in reference to another king, his "pomp is brought down to Sheol, and the noise of [his] viols" when the King of Babylon was destroyed (Is. 14.11), and how the cornet, flute, harp, sackbut, psaltery, dulcimer, and all kinds of music was sounded when the King of Babylon was elated (see Dan. 3). Evidently, the archangel at that time was made king and therefore he was given all these musical instruments by God.

"Thou wast the anointed cherub that covereth" (v.14a). "Anointed" means he was being set apart. The work of a "cherub" or "living creature" (cf. Ez. 10.15) is to lead in worshiping the Lord (see Rev. 4.9,10; 5.11–14). So that Lucifer's work at the beginning was to lead the creatures of that day in the worship of God. This also indicates he had the office of a priest.

"And I set thee, so that thou wast upon the holy mountain of God; thou hast walked up and down in the midst of the stones of fire" (v.14b). The mountain of God most probably is the place where the glory of God is manifested. Since he is God's priest, Lucifer would naturally stand before God and serve Him. What is the meaning of "walked up and down in the midst of the stones of fire"? According to Ezekiel 1.26, the place of the cherubim or "living creatures" (see Ez. 1.19ff.) is just beneath the throne

of God. When Moses and seventy of the elders of Israel were called to Mount Sinai, it says that "they saw
the God of Israel; and there was under his feet as it
were a paved work of sapphire stone, and as it were
the very heaven for clearness . . . And the appear-
ance of the glory of Jehovah was like devouring fire
on the top of the mount in the eyes of the children of
Israel" (Ex. 24.10,17). So that this paved work of sapphire stone which looked like devouring fire is "the
stones of fire" spoken of here in Ezekiel 28.14b. It
thus indicates that originally this archangel was placed
in the habitation of the Most High directly under the
throne of God where he was very close to God.

"Thou wast perfect in thy ways from the day that
thou wast created, till unrighteousness was found in
thee" (v.15). Whatever God created was perfect, because He is not the originator of sin. Unrighteousness
began with this sinful archangel Lucifer. He was created by God and was given a free will, just as God has
given us human beings free will. How sad that this
created angel misused this freedom! How many are
the people today who abuse their freedom even as
Satan of old did.

"By the abundance of thy traffic they filled the
midst of thee with violence, and thou hast sinned"
(v.16a). We may apply this word to the Antichrist,
since in the last days we know that commerce will be
greatly increased (see Rev. 18). Due to the increase in
trade, many sins also follow. This is easily proven by
observing past human history.

However, this word may also be applied to Satan.
Pember has pointed out that the word "traffic" may

also be translated "detraction" or "slander."* We know the word "devil" in the original means "slanderer," "calumniator" or "malignant accuser." How Satan accused Job and attacked him without mercy! At the end of this age we shall hear these words: "Now is come the salvation, and the power, and the kingdom of our God, and the authority of his Christ: for the accuser of our brethren is cast down, who accuseth them before our God day and night" (Rev. 12.10). The phrase "cast down" here corresponds to that of the "cast out" in Ezekiel 28, and the reason for his being cast out is likewise the same. Probably in Ezekiel God is seen as condemning Satan's sin, whereas in the Revelation passage He is observed as sending Michael to execute the judgment against Satan. Why does God allow Satan to remain in the air today? Possibly because (1) God's time is not yet come, and/or (2) there is still much rubbish in God's children which needs to be purified by means of this fiery furnace.

Verse 17 states explicitly the cause of Satan's fall: "Thy heart was lifted up because of thy beauty; thou hast corrupted thy wisdom by reason of thy brightness." The description given of the King of Babylon in Isaiah 14.12–14 is quite similar to what is described here with respect to Satan. Hence many of God's servants believe that what the Holy Spirit has said applied not only to the King of Babylon but in a deeper sense also applied to the one behind the King of Babylon, even Satan. It tells of the cause of Satan's fall. I

---

*G. H. Pember, *op. cit.,* p. 52.

believe Ezekiel reveals the *cause* of Satan's pride whereas Isaiah discloses how proud he *was*. It might be that inwardly as he compared himself to the other created beings of God, he began to be proud and arrogant. Later on he even thought of himself as being equal with God. Thus he incurred God's judgment: "How art thou fallen from heaven, O day-star, son of the morning! . . . And thou saidst in thy heart, I will ascend into heaven, I will exalt my throne above the stars of God; and I will sit upon the mount of congregation, in the uttermost part of the north; I will ascend above the heights of the clouds; I will make myself like the Most High" (Is. 14.12–14). Because of his arrogant pride, he was punished by God. All his powers in heaven were being taken away from him. (Since the prophecy which follows has nothing to do with our present investigation, we will end our consideration from Ezekiel at this point.)

From Lucifer to Satan: a Summary

Now if our interpretation is correct, we can readily see from this prophetic passage of Ezekiel how in the former world God created a most beautiful and intelligent archangel (Lucifer) whom He established as leader of that creation. God placed him in the Garden of Eden, a garden far more ancient and superior to that Eden of Adam's time. It might have looked something like what the future New Jerusalem shall be like. There in Eden the archangel was to function as prophet, using his wisdom to instruct all who inhabited the former world how to serve God. He was also the priest of God to lead them to worship and praise the Lord. Among the created beings of that day he was to serve as king, for his position was higher than all the rest of creation. He might have remained in this blessed state for quite a long while (please re-read verse 15); yet he sinned, and henceforth he became God's greatest enemy.

The Fallen Angels and Demons

We have now seen the origin of Satan. What about the angels under him and the demons? How did their fall affect the earth and help to turn it into waste and void?

From the New Testament we can trace two orders of Satan's subjects: (1) the angels, (2) the demons. Let us look at the angels first. "Depart from me, ye cursed, into the eternal fire which is prepared for the devil and his angels" (Matt. 25.41). "And his [the dragon's] tail draweth the third part of the stars of heaven" (Rev. 12.4). The "stars" here refer to the angels (cf. Rev. 1.20). The passage continues later with these words: "And the great dragon was cast down, the old serpent, he that is called the Devil and Satan, the deceiver of the whole world; he was cast down to the earth, and his angels were cast down with him" (v.9). These angels must be those spirits whom God had set in the beginning to assist the archangel to rule the world. They are "the gods" in Psalm 82.1 (cf. John 10.35). Now at the fall of Lucifer, these probably conspired with him—at least they were in sympathy with him. And so they fell into sin with

Satan and have now become the principalities, the powers, the world rulers of this darkness, and the spiritual hosts of wickedness in the heavenlies (Eph. 6.12). These angels are not disembodied demons. They have instead an ethereal body, for the Lord reveals to us the fact that in resurrection people will be as angels in heaven.

Satan has another order of subjects. These are the evil spirits or the demons. "When even was come, they brought unto him [Christ] many possessed with demons: and he cast out the spirits with a word, and healed all that were sick" (Matt. 8.16). Here the Holy Spirit uses these two words "demons" and "spirits" synonymously. Likewise in Luke 10.17,20: "And the seventy returned with joy, saying, Lord, even the demons are subject to us in thy name"; and the Lord answered as follows: "Nevertheless in this rejoice not, that the spirits are subject unto you; but rejoice that your names are written in heaven." Here the Lord Jesus considers "demons" and "spirits" to be the same. Again, Matthew 17.18 records how the Lord cast "the demon" out of a boy. Concerning the same incident, Mark refers to the demon as "the unclean spirit," a "dumb and deaf spirit" (9.25).

These demons or spirits probably were a pre-adamic race who inhabited the former world. They either assisted Satan in rebellion or else they followed him afterwards. And thus they were destroyed by God by their being disembodied. These beings have consequently become disembodied spirits. Though there is no plain evidence in the Scriptures, we can still find some hints in the Bible. For instance, in Matthew 12 there is the situation of such a spirit after it had left a human body: it "passeth through waterless places, seeking rest, and findeth it not" (12.43). It became helpless and, wandering far outside the human body, it could find no rest. Finally, it was compelled to re-enter the original place—the human body. If these beings are not in fact *disembodied* spirits, why must they enter a human body? Furthermore, in Luke 8 we read how unwilling the demon called Legion was to leave the human body. When they (those of the Legion) were pressed, they preferred to enter the bodies of the swine. These demons are different from Satan and his fallen angels because the latter have no desire to enter human bodies since they still retain their own ethereal bodies. The demons, on the other hand, are different. Both their character and desire seem to prove that they are indeed disembodied spirits. If that be true, though, when were they disembodied? We know that the spirits of the dead today are either in Paradise or in Hades. Where, then, came these spirits? They must have come from the former world. When they were living, their dwelling place must have been the world which Satan formerly governed.

That there were inhabitants in the former world can be deduced from another passage in the Scriptures. We have already pointed out from Isaiah 45.18 that the world—that is to say, the former world—was not created a waste but was formed to be inhabited. This seems to imply that there were inhabitants in the earth of old.

As we study the Bible further we discover even

more information regarding this matter. There is a place of detention for evil spirits today. The spirits called Legion who were among the Gerasene demoniacs knew about this place. This was why they were so terrified as to entreat the Lord "not [to] command them to depart into the abyss" (Luke 8.31).

Regarding the abyss, Pember wrote: "It is called the abyss; and in some passages, such as the ninth chapter of the Apocalypse, this term is evidently applied to a fiery hollow in the centre of the earth: but it is also used for the depths of the sea, a meaning which accords well with its derivation."* The book of Revelation informs us that one day Satan will be cast into this abyss (20.3). Evidently some of the demons are now imprisoned there, but some of them are still free, waiting for the appropriate time when they too will be shut in there. This abyss is most likely in the sea, not in the center of the earth. And at the time of the final judgment (see Rev. 20.11–15), all the prisoners will be cast into the lake of fire, and in the New Heaven and the New Earth there will be no more sea (Rev. 21.1). Probably there is only one abyss, but it is scattered in two places—at the center of the earth and in the depth of the sea.

We have even more allusion in the Scriptures to this detention center of the demons. According to the Greek Septuagint of the Old Testament the word "deep" in Genesis 1.2 is the same as the word "abyss" here in the Greek New Testament. We have already mentioned how these demons were probably

---

*G. H. Pember, *op. cit.,* p. 60.

the preadamic race who inhabited the former world. In reading Genesis 1.2 it looks quite reasonable to us that those who originally inhabited the earth had their bodies destroyed by God because of their sins, and the place in which they dwelt was also judged by God by being turned into waste and a void so that the whole earth was covered with water and became a deep sea. How natural it would be for the spirits of those former inhabitants to be shut into the depth of this sea! Later on, when God restored the earth on the third day, He commanded the land to appear out of the waters, and called the gathering together of the waters the Seas. This dry land, the earth, was ready for men of the new world.

Where then did these demons go? Naturally our answer would be, these demons were left with the sea. When we read Revelation 20.13 ("And the sea gave up the dead that were in it; and death and Hades gave up the dead that were in them") we understand how death and Hades will give up the dead, but we are often puzzled at how the sea will give up the dead in it. The common interpretation is that the sea will yield up the bodies of all who were drowned. Yet if that be so, the earth must also yield up its dead since more bodies will have been buried in the earth than in the sea. The earth, however, will not give up the dead. Consequently, what the sea will yield up cannot be the bodies of the dead people but the spirits already shut within it. Human souls are kept in death and Hades. The Bible never suggests that human souls are kept in the sea. Thus who can be the dead given up by the sea except those who belonged to the former world? The order here is quite revealing: "And the sea gave up the dead that were in it; and death and Hades gave up the dead that were in them." Those inhabitants of the former world died first, therefore they shall be delivered up first. People of our present world will follow next since all shall be judged in order of time.

We have briefly touched on the origin of Satan, his angels, and these demons. As to how the preadamic race lived on the former earth, this seems to be beyond our knowledge. Yet we can obtain some understanding through a few intimations in the Scriptures. Many Bible scholars, including C. I. Scofield, believe that Jeremiah 4.23–26 refers to the conditions of the waste and void cited in Genesis 1.2. Although what precedes and what follows speak of the desolations of Judah, these verses appear to take on a broader cast in that it seems that God showed His prophet the desolations of the original earth. If our interpretation is correct, then we know from this passage that there were "fruitful fields" and "cities" (v.26) in the former world. The early settlers dwelt in cities and cultivated the fields. The fierce anger of the Lord came upon them and upon the entire earth because of their rebellion with Satan. And thus the earth became waste and void.

A Summary

If our meditation together has been correct, then the conditions of the original world and the cause of its desolation may be summed up as follows: At the beginning of time (in contrast to eternity) God created the heavens and the earth. The earth was not at that time a waste and void (Is. 45.18) but was instead most beautiful. On that earth there were not a few inhabitants. Yet before God had created the earth and its preadamic race, He had created angels (see Job 38.6,7). Of the myriads of angels created, He set Lucifer as head. This archangel was fairer and wiser than all other created beings. He was a masterpiece of God's creative act. He dwelt in the ancient preadamic Garden of Eden and was given dominion over the world. And as a result he was called the prince of the world (John 14.30). Many angels were under his authority; they helped him to govern this world. But due to his position and glory, he became proud and rebellious. He wished to lift himself up to be equal with God. He was unhappy to be a created being and wished to be a creator. So he began to slander God before the preadamic race and to accuse the latter before God. His unrighteousness was found out, he was duly condemned, and at the fullness of time Lucifer was cast down from heaven to earth. One third of the angelic beings followed him in his rebellion, so that they became the devil's messengers. For them God has prepared hell (Matt. 25.41); and into hell shall Satan and his followers be cast at the appropriate time. The preadamic race who inhabited the former earth was under the rule of this archangel and his angels. That race was enticed and their sins became full (we can readily understand this situation by comparing it with our own world today). So that through the fierce anger of God the earth and all who inhabited it were destroyed. Many evil spirits were shut into the abyss of the sea. Satan, his angels, and the evil spirits thus compose the kingdom of darkness. We do not know how long such a condition continued on before God took new action.

But then the Spirit of God moved upon the face of the waters, and the triune God began to repair the world. And after He finished restoring the earth, He created Adam and Eve. He ordered them to be on guard that through the union of man with heaven the power of Satan might be put to nought. Adam, however, was tempted into sin, and he fell. Instead of subduing the world and bringing it back to God, he delivered the world which God had given him to Satan once again. Angels had earlier failed, and now man failed. So God himself came to be man as the Last Adam, even the Lord Jesus Christ.

The Lord Jesus has become the prophet, priest and king of God. On earth He was the spotless prophet of God. Towards the hour of His death, He could boldly declare that "the prince of the world cometh: and he hath nothing in me" (John 14.30). As He died, all who are in Adam were crucified in Him. Being God, He was able to have the old Adamic creation crucified in himself and to begin a new creation. Through His death and resurrection He recovered the world which the first Adam had lost. Thus sinners who deserve to die can die to the old Adam by His death and be joined in life to Him—that is to say, to the Christ. This is salvation and such is the meaning of believing in the death of the Lord Jesus. All who believe in the Lord are therefore at enmity with the devil. The latter will attack us in all things, yet we must resist him, his angels, and his demons at all times. And such is real spiritual warfare.

Thus, Satan was judged once at "the holy mountain of God" and once again at Calvary. His sin has already been condemned, and only the execution has not been fully carried out. The time will come when he shall be cast down to earth. And when the Son of God shall return to the earth, then Satan shall be cast into the abyss. And after a thousand years he will be thrown into the lake of fire to suffer eternally. Today, our Lord Jesus holds the keys of death and of Hades. He will wait until He wipes out all traces of rebellion. He has brought His own blood into the holiest of all, having purified the heaven, and ever since acting as the *priest* of God. At His return, all things shall be restored to God's original design. Then shall He be God's *King.* He with His overcoming saints shall rule this world from heaven. He shall instruct the inhabitants of the earth concerning the will of God and the way of worshiping Him. And the conditions of the millennial kingdom shall be similar to that of the world before sin entered in.

Having restored all things to their original design, Christ has fulfilled the eternal purpose of God. Then this world will be consumed by fire and a new heaven and a new earth will be created in which righteousness shall reign.

For this reason, we who are God's children ought to have a deeper sense of enmity toward the devil. In these thousands of years the one purpose of God has been for men to be united with Him in destroying the power of Satan. Our God is the One who cannot deny himself. The world which was lost through man He would not take back by himself. He therefore sent His Son to become a man, and as man to recover that which was lost. We, the saved ones, must work together with that unique Man, the Lord Jesus. We must resist the devil in our life, work, environment, and all things. We resist through faith (1 Peter 5.9) and not with fleshly weapons (2 Cor. 10.4).

How clever and beautiful was Satan before, but because of his pride he has fallen into such an irredeemable state. How dangerous are those people who consider themselves clever and beautiful! Beware, lest your pride and arrogance cause you to "fall into the condemnation of the devil" (1 Tim. 3.6). Pride and self-conceit are not the blessing of man; the fear of the great and incomparable Lord God is wisdom!

3 | Restoration of the Earth in Six Days

We have already seen how in the beginning God created a perfect world, but due to the sin of Satan and the preadamic race who inhabited the earth, both they and the earth they occupied came under God's judgment, and thus the earth became waste and void. Now we will see how God did the work of restoring the earth.

In the book of Job, the writer alludes to the defeat of Satan's rebellion to prove the foolishness of contending with God. "He [God] is wise in heart, and mighty in strength: who hath hardened himself against him, and prospered?—Him that removeth the mountains, and they know it not, when he overturneth them in his anger; that shaketh the earth out of its place, and the pillars thereof tremble; that commandeth the sun, and it riseth not, and sealeth up the stars" (9.4–7). When did God perform these great things? When did He ever shake the earth and seal the stars up because of men's hardness towards Him?

From the day of Adam onward, in our present world we have never seen God doing all these things. Hence what is described here must have reference to the time when God judged Satan and the world under his rule at his rebellion. It was then that God shook the earth out of its place so that the mountains were removed. Such a catastrophe came so swiftly that before the mountains were ever "aware," they were already removed. Not only the earth was shaken, even the celestial phenomena were affected. Under the judgment of God, the sun did not rise and the stars were sealed up, with the result that the whole world was plunged into utter darkness. And because there was no sunlight, there quite naturally was no heat: the earth entered into the glacial age. Only when God decided to restore the earth did the Spirit of God commence to move upon the face of the waters—that is to say, upon the face of the deep or of utter darkness.

Job mentioned not only the judgment of God, he also spoke of God's restoring work: "[He] that alone stretcheth out the heavens, and treadeth upon the waves of the sea; that maketh the Bear, Orion, and the Pleiades, and the chambers of the south; that doeth great things past finding out, yea, marvellous things without number" (9.8–10). "Stretcheth out the heavens" was the work which God did on the second day when He made the firmament to divide the waters above or beneath it. He called the firmament Heaven. "The waves [or heights] of the sea" (cf. mg.) might refer to the waters above the firmament. "Maketh the Bear, Orion, and the Pleiades, and the chambers of the south" could point to God's work done on the fourth day. Significantly the word "maketh" is not "create" since God here was not creating these stars but was merely remaking what He had formerly created. And for the record to say "sealeth up the stars" would doubtless indicate that the stars were already there. And thus the use of "maketh" would mean that God only restored the stars to the condition which obtained before their having been sealed up.

The First Day

Hence God commenced to do the work of restoration. Now because there was darkness upon the waters, He called light to shine forth. This illumination divided between light and darkness. In past years—and even up to today—many scoffers have laughed at the absurdity they thought they saw of there being light before the sun was ever created. With the advance of science, however, people can no longer scoff at the record of the Bible. Recent discoveries in science have borne witness to the accuracy of what Moses said. Although as we have said, Genesis is not a book of science nor is it to be used as a scientific text book, it nonetheless is not against science and does not contain any scientific error. Modern men know that besides the sun there are other sources of light. Light is a kind of energy which comes from unknown sources and produces some sort of unimaginable agitation in the ether which surrounds the universe. Though science still cannot tell us the source of this energy, faith knows and understands that when God said, "Let there be light," that "there was light" indeed! How sad that people would rather search in darkness than come to God who is the source of all things. They consider such faith in God's written record to be superstition—to be unscientific. Yet we who believe are glad because we have God as our Father.

It is not mentioned here that on the first day God created light. Before light was restored, God had confined the darkness to a definite area ("darkness was upon the face of the deep")—that is to say, only the earth. Since darkness had been limited to a definite area, light appeared merely to the whole of this dark area. So that when God said "Let there be light," He only commanded light to appear to this earth since the entire universe *was not all* in darkness.

At the time of Moses, science such as it was had no knowledge of any source of light except the sun. It was totally ignorant of cosmic rays such as the so-called Northern Lights. Yet Moses recorded the fact of God calling for light before He called for the sun. Unless he was inspired by the Holy Spirit, how could he have ever written so accurately? We thank God for He is not circumscribed by the ignorance of men. The more that scientists understand the natural laws set into the universe by God, the more they shall realize the trustworthiness of God's word.

"And God called the light Day, and the darkness he called Night. And there was evening and there was morning, one day" (1.5). When did the first day begin? Some think it started from the inception of the waste and void. But this could not be the meaning here: "there was evening and there was morning, one day." The "morning" must be the time in which light appeared. If there in fact had been no light before the first day, the term "evening" here would have no meaning whatsoever because the evening and the morning mentioned here were the explicit result of light. If indeed the word "evening" refers to the darkness found in verse 2, would not this evening be very, very long? Yet Genesis does not take the waste and void of verse 2 as being in the first day. So that before the "evening" of the first day, there must already have been light; otherwise, how would the evening and the morning be divided? The Bible does not say God *created* light on the first day; it merely records that God commanded light to shine. Where did this light come from? It could not have come from the earth since it was in waste and void and was encircled in darkness. It must have come from the original heavens which God had created in the beginning. This again proves that our present world is but a restored world.

The Six Days: Twenty-Four Hours Each

Let it be known that the Six Days are days of twenty-four hours each. The Bible does indeed sometimes use the term "day" to represent an extended *period* of time such as "the day of the Lord," etc. But the Six Days here are not to be construed as six prolonged periods. No unbiased readers will take them as being prolonged periods of time. We know each time the Bible uses the term "day" to stand for a period, it never qualifies that day with a number such as one, two, first, second, and so forth. But if a number *is* placed before the day, it invariably means the time the earth requires to make one revolution upon its axis. Now it is explicitly stated here that "there was evening, and there was morning, one day." And hence this must be a day of but twenty-four hours in length.

Furthermore, when later on God set apart the sabbath day, it is stated clearly that He rested on the seventh day; for when He commanded the children of Israel to remember the sabbath day, this is the way God phrased it: "Remember the sabbath day, to keep it holy. Six days shalt thou labor, and do all thy work; but the seventh day is a sabbath unto Jehovah thy God: . . . for in six days Jehovah made heaven and earth, the sea, and all that in them is, and rested the seventh day: wherefore Jehovah blessed the sabbath day, and hallowed it" (Ex. 20.8–11). Obviously for the children of Israel, all seven days represent days of twenty-four hours in length.

Suppose we *were* to take the Six Days as six long geological periods. What, then, would be "the evening" of these geological periods and what would be "the morning"? Before the third geological period, there would be no grass nor trees on earth. Before the sixth geological period, there could be no fossils of animals. The fact is that there is no such distinction of plants and animals to be found in earth's strata.

If the Six Days were indeed six prolonged periods, would not Adam who was created on the sixth day have lived in the Garden of Eden for a very long while before he had sinned? Moses who wrote Genesis actually had no idea of using the term "day" to signify a lengthy period. Let us not bend the word of God to suit our theory or to soften people's attack. For if we interpret the divine word according to our private opinion, we will subject the Scriptures to criticism as well as bring reproach to ourselves. On the basis of the evidences we have given above, it is certain that these Six Days are not six prolonged periods. Our God is almighty. Six twenty-four-hour days are quite enough for Him to restore the earth, so why should He need six lengthy periods? Since He was willing to repair the world in six days, let us observe His works with humility and praise Him for His majesty. We have absolutely no need to agree with the theory of the unregenerated. We know that what geology (if it is correct in its assumptions) demands can be met sufficiently during the period which lasted between the time of the first verse and that of the second verse of Genesis 1.

The Second Day

On the second day, God once more gave His order. He put the firmament in the air so as to divide the waters from the waters. He separated the waters under the firmament from the waters above the firmament. Science once again must appreciate this beautiful description. This is the effectiveness of the expanse or atmosphere. It divides the waters above and beneath it, and yet it is not inflexible. The firmament can contain moisture that can hang over us. It is not a solid reservoir which stores the waters in the sky since the "birds fly above the earth in the open firmament of heaven" (Gen. 1.20).

"And God called the firmament Heaven" (1.8a) This "heaven" is different from the "heavens" mentioned in verse 1. For in verse 1 the term "heavens" points to the universe and its fullness, whereas the "heaven" here refers only to the air or atmosphere above our earth. The heavens mentioned in the first verse have never been corrupted; only the earth and its celestial bodies were changed due to God's judgment. Concerning the Six Days of work, God pronounced each day's work as good except the second day. Did God forget? Not at all, for what He says or does *not* say is equally full of meaning. The Scriptures are God-breathed, word for word. He did not pronounce the second day's work good because the firmament or air is somewhat related to Satan. Is not Satan "the prince of the powers of the air" (Eph. 2.2), and are not the demons that are under him called "the spiritual hosts of wickedness in the heavenly places" (Eph. 6.12)? Seeing that this firmament would be the habitation of Satan and his evil spirits, God did not sum up this day's work as being good. Yet how did these evil spirits ascend to the air? We have already mentioned how they were detained in the depths of the sea, which was the waters here. Now as God divided the waters above and beneath the firmament, these wicked beings had the opportunity of escaping at the moment of the lifting of waters into the air where their prince dwelt. Hence the New Testament speaks of the evil spirits of the air who today work upon the earth. Though they are escaped convicts, they nevertheless are allowed to be free for a while till they shall be cast into the abyss. The air thus becomes the headquarters for the kingdom of darkness. Do we not notice that the works of Satan usually begin from the air? For this reason, while we are meeting or praying, we need to ask God to clear the air by means of the precious blood of our Lord so that we may not be oppressed by the enemy.

The Third Day

Even though the waters had been divided above and beneath the firmament, the earth at this point was still covered with water. There was yet no dry ground. On the third day, therefore, God once again commanded, this time saying: "Let the waters under the heavens be gathered together unto one place, and let the dry land appear: and it was so" (1.9). What is mentioned here agrees perfectly with the manner in which we have interpreted Genesis 1.1 and 1.2. The command of God was for the dry land to appear. By this we know that the land was already there, except that it was buried beneath the many waters and needed only to appear. For God did not say, "Let the dry land be created out of nothing"; He merely ordered the waters to recede to a certain place so that the land which He had created in the beginning might now appear. This further proves that the works of the Six Days were not creative but restorative in nature.

Psalm 104.5-9 describes how God in the beginning created the earth; then how He judged the earth; and finally how He bade the flood to subside—which was the work of the third day: (1) "Who laid the foundations of the earth, that it should not be moved for ever"—this segment of the passage in Psalm 104 refers to God's original creation. (2) "Thou coveredst it with the deep as with a vesture; the waters stood above the mountains"—this segment of the passage depicts the conditions of the earth which obtained after God had judged the earth, and thus coincides with the phrase "darkness [which] was upon the face of the deep" found in Genesis 1.2. And (3) "At thy rebuke they fled; at the voice of thy thunder they hasted away (the mountains rose, the valleys sank down) unto the place which thou hadst founded for them. Thou hast set a bound that they may not pass over; that they turn not again to cover the earth"—this segment has reference to the work of God performed during the first part of the third day. "Thy rebuke" and "the voice of thy thunder" are phrases which allude to God's command in Genesis. That the waters are said here to have "fled" and to have "hasted away" show further how "the waters under the heavens [were] gathered together unto one place" at God's command as recorded in Genesis. The words "the mountains rose, the valleys sank down" in no way imply that this was the beginnings of mountains and valleys since in verse 6 of this Psalm the mountains were already spoken of as existing. These words simply indicate how the mountains which were once covered by waters would now appear after the waters receded. And so "the dry land [did] appear" once again. Reading further in our Psalm 104 passage, we find these words: "Unto the place which thou hadst founded for them. Thou hast set a bound that they may not pass over; that they turn not again to cover the earth." These words describe in detail how the waters were "gathered together" by God "into one place" so that "the dry land" would "appear." Thus do we firmly believe that our present world is but what God has restored.

From the above discussion we see that the earth emerged from out of the waters. Yet this has also been attested by science, for geology today fully agrees with this fact. We are told that the geological strata were long ago formed in the waters.

Still on the third day, God had performed yet another work. When the land came out of the waters, there were no grass nor trees upon it. God therefore decorated the land with grass and fruit trees.

The Fourth Day

On the fourth day, God repaired the celestial bodies because the terrestrial conditions were by this time restored. On the first day, He had called forth light to shine; but on this day He made the "lights." We know that the light on the first day had already divided night from day (vv.4,5); now the function of the "lights" were also to divide night from day (v.16). Thus there is a similarity in function between the "light" of the first day and the "lights" of the fourth day. Probably the light of the first day shone on one side of the earth half a day and on the other side of the earth half a day. So that there was night and day on the first day. On the fourth day, God made the "lights" or light-holders to contain the light. As our earth rotates in relation to these light-holders, the latter serve "for signs, and for seasons, and for days and years."

The greater light which God made is the sun. It does not say here that God "created" the sun because it had been created in the beginning. Here it was merely being "repaired." Possibly the preadamic world had also the sun as light-holder. After the rebellion of Satan, though, the sun was affected and, being surrounded by darkness, it failed to shine. Nevertheless, our earth continued to rotate around the sun. But on the fourth day, God repaired the sun and caused it to be a light-holder again.

Scientists tell us that the moon is a barren desert waste. It is not hard to conceive that the sun, moon and stars were all evilly affected by the rebellion of Satan.

After God had "made the two great lights," He also made "the stars." Let us again reiterate that these stars were not created at this time because they already existed. We can prove this from the book of Job: "Where wast thou when I laid the foundations of the earth? . . . Who determined the measures thereof, . . . or who stretched the line upon it? Whereupon were the foundations thereof fastened? Or who laid the corner-stone thereof, *when the morning stars* sang together . . .?" (38.4–7) Whether the earth spoken of here refers to the original creation or the restoration of the third day, one thing is nonetheless certain, which is, that before the earth was made, there already were the stars. For when the earth was in the making, the morning stars already "sang together" about the works of God. So that here on the fourth day God was merely making an adjustment to the stars which He had created before. Now since He placed so much light in the sun, God quite logically called it the greater light. And then He caused the stars to appear in the horizon to meet the need of the earth.

When God inspired Moses to write, He enabled the latter to describe His works with *human* needs in view because the Bible has been given to men to read. He did not show us the other uses of these sun, moon and stars but only their use to men. Even so, because these are "for signs, and for seasons, and for days and years," they do have a relationship to other created things as well, yet the fact they are "for signs" is especially significant for mankind because none except humanity would regard heavenly phenomena as signs. The places and positions of sun, moon and stars have likewise been determined through ordinary human observations. According to mankind, the sun is the greater light, the moon the lesser light, and the individual stars even lesser lights than the moon. How wonderful that God should provide us humble men with such a vast world!

The Fifth Day

On the fifth day God prepared and created living things to inhabit the earth which was already restored. "Let the waters swarm with swarms of living creatures, and let birds fly above the earth in the open firmament of heaven'' (1.20). This was God's command, which represented His thought. "And God created the great sea-monsters, and every living creature that moveth, wherewith the waters swarmed, . . . and every winged bird . . . (v.21) This shows how God created them out of nothing. We do not know with what new materials God created fishes and the other living creatures of the waters. We do know, however, through Genesis 2.19, that the birds were made out of the ground. Science informs us that living creatures existed in the waters before they appeared on the land. Aquatics are the earliest species of such living creatures. Even today there are still large families of living creatures in the seas. Birds are an earlier species among warm-blooded creatures. How much in agreement the findings in science and the statements in the Bible are.

The Sixth Day

On the sixth day man was created. He was created according to God's image. In the first chapter of Genesis it mentions simply the creation of man to indicate his position among the created beings. Only in Chapter 2.7–15 is the origin of man described in detail to indicate his relationship with God.

Let us notice that man was "created" (1.27) by God. He was not "evolved" from the lower animals. We have previously explained this word "created" to mean a calling into being from nothing. This is a distinct act of God and not the result of natural selection. The Bible never endorses the theory of evolution, which remains forever only a theory. Let us consider the following events. On the third day God ordered that "the earth [bring] forth grass, herbs yielding seed *after their kind*" (v.12). Herbs cannot become trees, nor trees change to be herbs. On the fifth day "God created the great sea-monsters, and every living creature that moveth, wherewith the waters swarmed, *after their kind,* and every winged bird *after its kind*" (v. 21). And on the sixth day "God made the beasts of the earth *after their kind*, and the cattle *after their kind,* and everything that creepeth upon the ground *after its kind.*" (v. 25). Each and every species of created being is *after its kind.* Though the Bible does not tell us how these species are divided, nevertheless, the phrase "after its kind" at least proves that all that were created are after their kind. Since God has said "after their kind" or "after its kind," He has clearly ordained the boundary of each kind. There is no possibility of one kind evolving into another. Not only is it impossible for a plant to become an animal, it is also impossible for one species of plant to become another species of plant or one species of animal to become another species of animal.

We Christians believe in the word of God. Without a "thus saith the Lord" we will believe nothing. How can we believe anything which is contradictory to God's word? His word is sufficient to solve all problems. People of the world may ridicule what they deem to be our foolish logic, but we are satisfied with God's word. How sad that people do not believe in our God and so they wander aimlessly. They even create for themselves a kind of teaching in which they place their faith. They conclude that for God to create out of nothing and to form man from the red earth is too much of a wonder in which to believe. Yet is it not even a more incredible proposition to have to believe in, as many men do, to believe that a microscopic seed evolves through many species until it becomes an ape and then finally evolves into a man? Is not this even far more exceedingly unbelievable a thing than for God to create man? I would therefore wish to warn people not to believe in such absurdity which has been propounded in these last days. We must not believe in it or even listen to it. We should not heed those books and magazines which advocate such false teaching.

We thank God for the simplicity of His word. He said "after their kind" and "after its kind." We do not observe any plant or animal before our eyes which does not obey the word which God had spoken. Earlier the evolutionists had said how millions of years ago our ancestors had been certain creeping things or animals. Now they tell us that millions of years into the future our progeny will become a kind of creature without fingers or toes. Whether they talk of millions of years before or beyond our current day, we shall never see what they claim or predict, and therefore we have no way to argue with them. The Bible, though, is a current book. It never makes an irresponsible statement. None of the created beings disobeys the law enunciated in Genesis of being "after its kind."

We are told that the word "God" (*Elohim*) is a

uni-plural noun which always is followed by a singular verb. It is rather unusual for a plural noun to be conjoined to a singular verb. But this is used to express the trinity of God. Because in the Godhead there is more than one person, no singular noun can be used. *Elohim* in that sense is a collective noun; it speaks of three in one, not of three Gods; hence it takes a singular verb. Though the Bible never says plainly that God is triune, there are nonetheless plenty of proofs and hints in it to support this truth. The doctrine of the Trinity is a major teaching of the holy Scriptures which we need not question. Furthermore, in Genesis 1.26 ("And God said, Let us make man in our image, after our likeness") the word "us" reveals the plurality of the Godhead while the word "make" shows the unity of God's will. In the first chapter of Genesis the phrase "God said" is used 31 times. What God says is His "Word," and as we read John chapter 1 we learn that the world was made by the "Word" of God. So that even in Genesis 1 the creative work of the Lord Jesus (who is the Word) is already being mentioned. We witness in Genesis 1 how the triune God worked together in creation. "God," "God said," and "the Spirit of God"— Father, Son, and Holy Spirit—were all present.

Now before God created man, there was a pause. There was a council among the Godhead, and the decision was: "Let us make man in our image, after our likeness; and let them have dominion . . ." (v.26). In pondering upon this divine council we can understand how carefully God worked. Due to the failure of

Satan and the preadamic race, the earth became waste and void. Then God restored the earth and its heaven to be habitable. All the living creatures were now made and ready. But then a pause. And then a conversation among the Godhead: "Now let us make man!" Such is the spirit of the word of God here.

Yet what is the purpose in creating men? "Let them have dominion," we are told by the Godhead. Satan has failed, he can no longer rule the world. Though he is yet free, he is under the judgment of God because his sin has already received its sentence. The earth which God has restored is to have nothing to do with Satan. It is to be a new order. In spite of the possibility of Satan retaining his title as "the prince of the world," the man whom God created has a free will—that is to say, he has his sovereignty. For God appointed man—outside the power of Satan—to rule over the newly recovered earth and all the plants and animals on it. If man could preserve the sovereignty which he received from God, Satan would merely hold on to an empty title. For God intended to destroy the power of Satan through man.

Now we know it would be very easy for God by himself to destroy the devil. We therefore do not know why God would rather have man to work with Him in destroying the works of the devil. Nevertheless, God proceeded to make man and to give him dominion. This office was lost to Satan, and yet, alas, very soon we witness the fall of man. Man loses his sovereignty, and the devil regains the power and reign of his title as "the prince of the world." In chapter 3 of Genesis, to be discussed later, we shall see more of this. But suffice it for us for now to know that God has only one purpose in His counsel and works´ regarding this world, and that is, to destroy the power of Satan. The Lord Jesus called Satan the enemy (see Matt. 13.39). We believers who have been chosen by the Lord should therefore never forget this purpose of our being involved in destroying the works and the power of the devil. Whatever we do, we should not ask if this matter is good or bad but ask instead if it is *profitable to God* and *destructive to Satan.* We will not do anything if it has no power to affect the kingdom of darkness and to cause damage to the devil.

In all our works we are to judge them not by the apparent result but by the effect they shall have in the spiritual realm as to who will gain and who will lose. This is spiritual warfare that is not to be waged by the efforts of flesh and blood. This is also to be the criterion at the judgment seat on that day: whether a work is to be burned or to stand shall be based on how effective it was in effecting the will of God. (The best way to attack the power of darkness is on the one hand to resist the works of Satan in the Spirit and deny him the victory, and on the other hand to use prayer as a weapon by asking God to destroy all the works and wiles of Satan. Positively, let us do the will of God. For each time we do His will, Satan suffers loss.)

On that sixth day man was created in God's image and after His likeness. This does not refer exclusively to the flesh, it instead shows that man is in a position to represent God on earth since he bears a similarity to God in both mind and morals, thus enabling him to know God and to communicate with Him. Unfortunately, through sinning he lost the image and likeness of God. The foolishness of man towards God today is beyond comprehension. And except he is born anew from above, he will never know how to converse with God. In the New Testament Paul has told us that man "is the image and glory of God" (1 Cor. 11.7). For when God created man, He created him to represent His own glory. To whom was the glory to be shown? To Satan who resides in the air. But the first man failed. The Second Man did not fail, however, for He being "the very image of his [God's] substance" (Heb. 1.3), Christ Jesus was able to fully represent God.

"And God said, Behold, I have given you every herb yielding seed, which is upon the face of all the earth, and every tree, in which is the fruit of a tree yielding seed; to you it shall be for food: and to every beast of the earth, and to every bird of the heavens, and to everything that creepeth upon the earth, wherein there is life, I have given every green herb for food" (1.29,30). In the world before sin entered in, meat was not eaten. Only in the sinful world has meat become a necessity. In the future—in the new heaven and the new earth—aside from eating the fruit of the tree of life, there is no record of eating any meat at all. The will of God for us today is: "For every creature of God is good, and nothing is to be rejected, if it be received with thanksgiving: for it is sanctified through the word of God and prayer" (1 Tim. 4.4,5). In this world of ours which is full of evil, "to abstain from meats'' (4.3) is to deny that the world is under a curse.

"And God saw everything that he had made, and, behold, it was very good'' (v.31). God never made anything bad. All things bad come from sin and not from God's creation. We who live in this evil world should not murmur against God, because in Him there is no evil and nothing bad ever came from His creative hands. On the contrary, God treated mankind with utmost kindness. He prepared the grass and herbs on the third day as food for man, the animals and birds—whom He then made on the fifth and sixth days. He made ready the environment before He put us in it. If we truly see this touch of kindness, what comfort it can be to us! God always provides for His creatures. Before the grass, He prepared the earth; before the animals, He prepared the plants. Sometimes we grow fearful because we fail to see God and His goodness. But how blessed are those with faith! For nothing can shake their hearts!

God's Sabbath

Chapter 2.1–3 should really be an extension of chapter 1. On the seventh day God finished His work and rested. One thing worth noticing here is that the rest mentioned is *God's* rest, not man's. The Bible declares that this is God's sabbath. God had worked for six days, and now He rested. This rest, however, was not physical, because God is never tired: "Hast thou not known? hast thou not heard? The everlasting

God, Jehovah, the Creator of the ends of the earth, fainteth not, neither is weary" (Is. 40.28). What, then, is the meaning of His rest? It is not physical but spiritual in nature. It signifies God's satisfaction. As He looked at what He had made and saw that all of it was very good, He was satisfied. All who study the Scriptures carefully should understand the meaning of God's rest. He had not set up the sabbath for man to keep, for man had done no work yet and therefore had no need to rest. Only after Adam sinned did he begin working (Gen. 3.19). Before he had sinned, Adam did not need to rest on the seventh day. Therefore, today we neither keep the sabbath of the children of Israel (for such belongs to the law) nor keep the sabbath of God's creation (for He had not given this day to man).

Another matter calls for our attention. With respect to the six preceding days it was always recorded that "there was evening and there was morning"; on this seventh day—the day of rest—there is no such record. After God had finished His work, He rested in the eternal day which is always day and never night. This rest is a type of the eternal rest (Heb. 4.3) in which all who labor with God shall rest eternally in that unending nightless day. The very thought of this should make our hearts glad.

4 | Creation and Christian Experience

We have seen how in the beginning God created the heavens and the earth, how the earth later turned to be waste and void, and how finally God restored the earth and its inhabitants in Six Days' work and then rested in satisfaction on the seventh day. Let us now meditate on the spiritual meaning we can draw from the story. For is the purpose of God in recording the story merely to inform us as to how He created and then remade the world? Or does He have a deeper thought behind it? Is there any similarity between our "new creation" and the creation of the original world? Is there any analogy between the creation of the physical world and that of the spiritual world? Is not the outer world of things a reflection of the inner world of the Spirit? We shall come to see, I believe, that the way God treats the universe and the way He deals with each individual person is very much alike. The procedure involved in the creation of the physical world reflects in God's plan and work the experience of personal renewal. The history of creation typifies the course of our life in the new creation.

What we shall thus focus on will not be the ancient and modern history of mankind but on the current experience of an individual. The greatest error of our modern age is to pay too much attention to mankind in general while neglecting in particular the individual who is his own self. Not so, though, with God. Although He means to bless mankind, He starts out with the individual. He does not despise any person. "Are not two sparrows sold for a penny? and not one of them shall fall on the ground without your Father" (Matt. 10.29). We ought to see the Father's hand in all His works. Man has indeed sinned and fallen, but thank God He does not despise anyone. How He pours out His heart towards every person. And such should be our comfort. Only God's heart can ever truly satisfy man's heart.

One

"In the beginning." This is the beginning of the world. "In the beginning God created the heavens and the earth" (v.1). How beautiful were the heavens and the earth as they came forth from the hand of the Creator. How perfect, pure, and fresh were the conditions of the original world. At that moment "the morning stars sang together, and all the sons of God shouted for joy" (Job 38.7). There was not the slightest trace of any murmuring or sighing mixed in with this joyful song. How harmonious were the Creator and His creation! There was no sin, no Satan, no sorrow, no pain, no sickness, and no leakage. Everything was prosperous. It was truly like a paradise.

Was not the original condition of man like this too? Was not the primal state of Adam and Eve as perfect as was the beginning of the physical world? Adam was created in God's image and after His likeness. Then God prepared for him a companion and placed them both in the Garden of Eden. God blessed them, committed all things into their hands, and made them together the prince of the world. God commanded them to be fruitful and multiply and replenish the earth. God called them very good. Adam had within him no inherent sinful nature, nor did he bear any mark of sin in his body.Even his surroundings had no vestige of sin. He was in fact an ideal man living in an ideal environment. He and his companion held constant communication with God. Everything made his heart glad.

Two

"[But] the earth [became] waste and void, and darkness was upon the face of the deep" (v.2a). The original, perfect world had fallen. A great catastrophe had come. The earth went through a tremendous change. The work of the Creator was now destroyed. The vessel in the potter's hand was broken, the beauty of the past had turned into ugliness. The good of the former days changed into corruption. What had originally been perfect sank into desolation. The sound of songs was no longer heard, and the light was now extinguished. The earth was drowned in the waters of God's judgment and darkness covered the face of the deep. Apart from the deadly colors, the salty smell, and the sound of the mighty breakers, there were no other phenomena. The earth originally created by God was in total ruin.

Is this not a realistic picture of the condition of man after he left God? What confusion, what darkness! The waves of passions and lusts roll constantly over one another. Beautiful personality is now sunk beneath the depth of sin, for "the wicked are like the troubled sea; . . . it cannot rest, and its waters cast up mire and dirt" (Is. 57.20).

Man had thus fallen. Formerly he had been blessed; now he is cursed. Death and sorrows descended upon his life and happiness because he was now deeply sunk in transgressions without any means of extrication, and enwrapped in darkness without any possibility of self-enlightenment. Such desolation as this is a symptom of fallen life. Darkness in morality and spirituality (see Eph. 4.18) is the common lot of sinners. "Waste and void, and darkness upon the face of the deep" is in truth an accurate description of a sinful man. How pitiful that many do not know themselves!

Such is the cause of all the tribulations and vexations in the world. Such is the reason for the evil nature of man. He has lost his position: "Therefore, as through one man sin entered into the world, and death through sin," even so, "as through the one man's disobedience the many were made sinners" (Rom. 5.12,19). The condition of man before God is now "waste and void and darkness." This is because man is "alienated from the life of God" (Eph. 4.18) and is "dead through [his] trespasses and sins" (Eph. 2.1). He is truly "exceedingly corrupt" (Jer. 17.9), for "all have sinned, . . . there is none that doeth good, . . . there is none righteous" (Rom. 3.23, 12,10). How sad that people of this world still brag about their knowledge, wisdom, learning and culture! It would be a blessing in disguise to them if they knew they were "waste and void and [full of] darkness"!

Three

"And the Spirit of God moved upon the face of the waters" (v.2b). Such waste and void and dark situation gave God no rest. Earth's subjection to sin, death and Satan gave Him no joy. It would be no surprise if God had given up on this fall and desolation. Yet what God did was really beyond expectation, for why *should* He be concerned anymore with that which He had judged? Why *should* He be mindful of this ruin, chaos, and corruption? Why *should* He care any further for this insignificant waste and void? Such questions are hard to answer. The only reply must be the mercy and the grace of God. God's mercy comes upon those who deserve no mercy, and God's love falls upon those who are not worthy to be loved. The desolate world and the fallen mankind have no right to ask God to work anew. From their point of view it would be a delusion for them to make such a request to God on their own. How could they at all expect God to be merciful to them? Yet in spite of man's unfitness and unworthiness, despite man's fall and failure, God's sovereign grace is poured out upon unfit and unworthy man and His boundless mercy and love falls upon fallen and failing humanity.

The first step of God's work is to have His Spirit "move upon the face of the waters." Otherwise, how can the earth ever be restored? How can the dead one raise himself? How can darkness transform itself into light? How can that which was judged by God's righteousness cause itself to receive again the blessing of God? Except for the working of the Holy Spirit, the fallen creation cannot lift itself up. How helpless and hopeless is the ruined and failing creation. No revival, recovery or resurrection is possible without the work of the Holy Spirit. And hence the fallen one must give up his own struggling and striving and humbly acknowledge that in himself, that is, in his flesh, there dwells no good thing (Rom. 7.18).

But praise and thank God, although a sinner cannot cause himself to be born anew even as the earth could not restore itself—although he cannot deliver himself from sin even as the earth could not free itself from the waters—and although he cannot practice righteousness even as the earth could not change darkness into light, God himself nevertheless undertakes the work of redemption for us. The new creation as well as the old creation is all the work of God. Just as man cannot create the world, so he cannot create his own spirit. The Lord must do *all* the work himself and thank God He did. Yet this was not

His duty for He had no obligation whatsoever to save us. He nonetheless saves us out of his unexpected grace. He need not do it, and yet He does it. That is mercy. Man does not deserve it and yet he receives it. That is grace. In salvation man stands absolutely in the place of a receiver. If he thinks he has any virtue, he blasphemes God and defies God's grace.

The work of the Holy Spirit here commences the regeneration of man. "Moved" in the original means "hovered" or "brooded" over. This meaning reveals a picture of lovingkindness and sensitivity. It is the same word used in Deuteronomy 32.11 in describing a mother eagle with her eaglets; and how God is the same: "As an eagle that stirreth up her nest, that fluttereth over her young, he *spread abroad* his wings, he took them, he bare them on his pinions." May we respond to the love of God! How His heart does desire after us! And who are we? Nobody but sinners—nobody but fallen men! Yet He is not angry at us, nor does He despise or forsake us. He does not consider us who are but "waste and void and darkness" as being unworthy for the Holy Spirit to brood over. "Thou that art of purer eyes than to behold evil, and that canst not look on perverseness" (Hab. 1.13). To think that God should humble himself to save those who are but dust and ashes. O God, "what is man, that thou art mindful of him? And the son of man, that thou visitest him?" (Ps. 8.4) We do not understand why God should love sinners such as we. I do not know why God should love me! Indeed, it is "not that we loved God, but that he loved us" (1 John

4.10). O God, Your grace is truly wonderful! Without any questioning on Your part, Your "delight was with the sons of men" (Prov. 8.31)!

God's love is the cause of our regeneration. "For God so *loved* the world . . . that whosoever believeth on him should not perish, but have *eternal life*" (John 3.16). The love of God constrains Him to work on the desolation and once again make it "very good." For unless such human desolation is restored to be "very good" once more, God's loving heart will never be able to rest!

Regeneration is the first and also the most essential work. Without this effort the light of God will shine on nothing. Hence God causes His Spirit to do the incomprehensible work in man as a preparation for His light: "Ye must be born anew. The wind bloweth where it will, and thou hearest the voice thereof, but knowest not whence it cometh, and whither it goeth: so is every one that is born of the Spirit" (John 3.7,8).

What a sinner actually lacks is none other than life. There is nothing in the world that can substitute for life. He does not want God, nor does he desire the light of God that is in the face of Jesus Christ. He hates as well as rejects the light: "The light is come into the world, and men loved the darkness rather than the light; for their works were evil. For every man that doeth evil hateth the light, and cometh not to the light, lest his works should be reproved" (John 3.19,20). Only the regenerated love light. And once a person is born again, he immediately becomes sensitive to God's light. His conscience is moved to turn towards God.

Four

"And God said, Let there be light: and there was light" (v.3). The preceding verse reads that "the Spirit of God moved"; here it reads: "And God said" (which is the word of God). God's Spirit and God's word work together and are inseparable. The Holy Spirit first works, then the word of God also works. We are "born of the *Spirit*" (John 3.5,6); and have been "begotten again, not of corruptible seed, but of incorruptible, through the *word* of God, which liveth and abideth" (I Peter 1.23). "The opening of thy words giveth *light*" (Ps. 119.130); therefore "God said," and "there was light."

In the first day's work, God used the Word to call forth light. The primary work of God's Spirit and God's Word is to send light into darkness. Sin has so darkened man's mind that if he is left alone he will have no knowledge of himself as to how dangerous his position is and that perdition awaits him in the future. From the spiritual standpoint, he is completely in the dark for he does not even know he needs a Savior. Neither his affection nor his reasoning will give him any light. But now the light of God comes. It shines into his heart. It actually sheds its light on the ruinous scene and reveals the fallen state of the creature. Nothing is changed except the darkness has been dispelled. None of the things revealed under the light can satisfy God's heart. The only thing good to God is His own light (v.4). In man there is absolutely nothing which can please God. But God loves His Son (see Matt. 3.17) because His Son is the true light (John 1.9). When the apostle Paul mentioned the first day of God's work, this is what he said: "Seeing it is God, that said, Light shall shine out of darkness, who shined in our hearts, to give the light of the knowledge of the glory of God in the face of Jesus Christ" (2 Cor. 4.6). Just as God's light shone upon the formerly dark world, even so, the Christ of God now shines upon the darkened heart of a sinner.

Now the moment man receives this divine enlightening, then "God divides the light from the darkness." Spiritual sensitivity and knowledge is now going to be gradually restored. What a person had previously considered good he now reckons bad; and vice versa. Though many still lack the experience of accurate discernment, they have nonetheless actually tasted the division of light from darkness. For at this time the work of God (through the light such work gives) has already begun the work of dividing man's enlightened spirit from his darkened soul (Heb. 4.12). Henceforth there is in man the division between "that which is born of the flesh [being] flesh; and that which is born of the Spirit [being] spirit" (John 3.6). Although such dividing has not reached its perfection because the believer does not have such a total experience, the fact of the matter is that such division now exists.

God divided the light from the darkness and gave each its name as well as its place. Darkness was still darkness, it forever being dark and never being able to turn into light. The earth itself is not a source of light. Whenever it turns its back to light, its condition remains dark. But as light shines into darkness, the light is not in any way affected by darkness. While light dispels darkness and gloom, nonetheless darkness still exists. In just the same way, man's old nature (the flesh) and man's old life (the soul life) is always dark. But when the spiritual life in a man grows strong, the old life and nature lose their power. Yet if one does not walk in the light, he will once again act in darkness. As long as we live in this world, and although we may walk continuously in the light, we shall nonetheless never be able to eliminate darkness or to eradicate our sinful life and nature. Because we are sons of light and sons of the day (see 1 Thess. 5.5), we must constantly walk in God's light or else darkness will encroach upon us and eventually overtake us once again.

Strictly speaking, day is not all light since it is the composite of both "evening" and "morning" (v.5). The highest life we can live in this world is "day"; yet it is imperfect because it consists of the combination of "evening" and "morning." If we say there is only morning and no evening in that life, that is not the "day" mentioned in the Scriptures. "If we say that we have no sin, we deceive ourselves" (1 John 1.8)—"If we say that we have not sinned, we make him [God] a liar, and his word is not in us" (1 John 1.10).

Even though darkness itself is "night," yet once it has been enlightened, it is no longer night but is "evening"; for no matter how dark such night is, it cannot be without some trace of light since it has the light of God shining upon it. Night cannot remain night but has become "evening" once it has been enlightened. In like manner, sometimes even to a believer who has been enlightened by God, his darkness may seem to make itself evident, except that what he manifests is not total "night" but is instead "evening." This is because, although his darkness remains in him without changing its nature, it is now under the control of the light. In spite of the fact he at times does fail and fall, he does not for this reason lose the light he has nor the life he receives and revert to being an unbelieving sinner once again. As one believes in the Lord Jesus, he is born again and possesses eternal life. Though he falls, he is still a son of God. He may "be overtaken in any trespass" (Gal. 6.1), but he has not returned to the place of an unregenerate sinner. How great is the grace of God!

"There was evening, and there was morning." This sentence is repeated six times in this first chapter of Genesis. Notwithstanding the fact that light is called "Day," what each of the Six Days come into is but "morning." The experience of the "Day" in its most perfect sense is yet to come. Morning is the foretoken of the day; it is not the full light of the day. In God's ordering, morning follows the night. Though we do have the dawning light, nevertheless, for it to shine more and more until the perfect day is an experience which still lies in the future. What we have now is only morning. The "Day" is when God's work shall be done and His heart shall be *fully* satisfied. He shall rest, and "the perfect day" shall have come (see Prov. 4.18). Then there will be no more evening and morning. We shall enter into God's rest, into the nightless day of everlasting joy. "Day unto day uttereth speech, and night unto night showeth knowledge" (Ps. 19.2). How few are those who hear!

Truly, the light we have today is only "morning." For us to shine in complete brightness is something yet in the future. When that which is limited is past, we shall enter into the perfection of God.

Five

"And God said, Let there be a firmament in the midst of the waters, and let it divide the waters from the waters" (v.6). This refers to the sky above us. This firmament divides the waters under and above it. What had been salty, dark waters have now evaporated and have ascended into the sky. What a division this is! By means of the "firmament" God divided the pure from the impure, and He caused them to stay in their respective places.

Such is a picture of the work of the cross. For its work is to divide. When the light of God shines on the face of the deep, it exposes the real condition of the waters. These boundless waters of bitterness were at one time wrapped in darkness so that no one could see its real face. But now the light has come. There is no hiding anymore. The brighter the light of God, the dirtier the waters appear to be. The light does not cleanse, it instead manifests the shame of man. What sorrow and what repentance ensues when one is under the light of God! That in which one took comfort in the past is now proven to be worthless. Not until this moment does he see the ugliness of his sinful life and nature. In dust and ashes he comes to know the dividing power of God's cross. The cross crucifies our sin (Rom. 6.6,11), self (Gal. 2.20), the flesh (Gal. 5.24), the world (Gal. 6.14), and the rudiments of the world (Col. 2.20). Separation by death is truly a great separation. It is a tremendous emancipation and an immense deliverance. Death cuts off all relationships; it terminates all complications. Apart from the cross there is nothing else which can sever us from that which is "under." In union with the death of Christ, we are delivered from all which is "under." Though we are born again, we are still held by our sin, self, flesh, the world, and its customs, all of which pull us downward. But after we experience co-death with Christ, we shall be a "separated" people. Once the light of God has led us to self-examination, this in turn will lead us to the cross that we may be delivered. The mark of the cross proves that we are a heavenly people, we now being separated from the world.

Do not confuse our position with our experience. As soon as we believe in the Lord Jesus as our Savior, our position in Him reaches the very peak. All He has accomplished for us is ours. He by His cross has divided that which is "above" from that which is "under." And this is our position. At that time, however, we may not yet have had the experience of such dividing between the "above" and the "under." It waits for us to exercise faith in accepting what He has accomplished on the cross and in joining ourselves to

His death before we can experience the deliverance from the things which are below and come into the experience of thinking on the things which are above. In spite of the fact that we have been "born from above" (John 3.3,7), we may not have yet experienced being "not of this world" (John 8.23). We must therefore "enter" into the Lord's death in experience so that we may truly know experimentally the dividing between our soul and spirit (Heb. 4.12). As the knife of the high priest cuts and divides the joints and marrow, so the work of the cross divides our spirit and soul.

The moment we are born again we are reckoned by God as having been crucified with Christ. Since we believe that Christ died for us, His death is therefore our death. This is co-death. Substitutionary death naturally produces co-death. Substitutionary death *is* co-death. As God accepts the substitutionary death of Christ, He reckons us as dead. Though in personal experience it is substitutionary death, under the eye of the law it is co-death. Hence, at the time we believe in the Lord Jesus we are in fact dead with Him. Nevertheless, we are still to experience this co-death. For the experience of co-death is obtained only after we are born again and after we seek deliverance through the cross as a result of the conflict between the two natures of light and darkness.

Now there is not only separation concerning outward things, there is also separation with respect to the inward condition. As God works secretly in human hearts, He causes man's affection and desire to turn to the things above. A man has been born

again, so he possesses the nature of God (2 Peter 1.4).
The cross enables this divine nature to divide the
things which are above from the things which are
below. It is this nature of God that reveals the difference. Today the believer's heart is inclined towards
heaven. The salty, dark passions and lusts are now
being cleansed so that the believer can think on the
things above.

Possessing physical life, man needs the air to supply life's breathing. By the same token, since the soul
has been illuminated by the heavenly light, it cannot
but breathe the heavenly air. God not only divides the
waters above and below the firmament, He also separates things within the soul. He thus puts "heaven" in
us and puts us in "heaven." The first sign of the saints
is that they belong to heaven. They have received a
heavenly calling, they serve the kingdom of the heavens, and they expect to enter the heavenly city. Since
their expectation is heaven, they wait for the heavenly
country, reckoning themselves to be sojourners and
strangers on the earth. After we have "heaven" both
within and without, we will know what are the things
above and what are the things below.

The inward heaven demands an outward heaven.
Having the heavenly life, we must have a heavenly
walk. The nature of the regenerated person is in terms
of "not walking in the counsel of the wicked" and
not just in terms of not "standing in the way of sinners, nor sitting in the seat of scoffers" (see Ps. 1.1).
The pleasures, delights and fashions of this world
cannot entrap him. Just as a healthy body must not
breathe in polluted air, a saint must not breathe in an

atmosphere of wickedness, jesting and confusion. He will rather love the presence of the brethren because they are his companions in the heavenly pilgrimage. "We know that we have passed out of death into life, because we love the brethren" (1 John 3.14).

By this time (that of vv.6–8) the heart of the believer has already come under God's control. Even so, his actual condition is not greatly different from that of his former state because the dry ground has not yet appeared in his life and the fruits have not been produced. Nevertheless, his heart is now turned upward, and the communion of heaven and man has already begun. With but one more step he shall be able to bear fruit to the glory of God.

Six

"And God said, Let the waters under the heavens be gathered together unto one place, and let the dry land appear: and it was so" (v.9). This is the third day of God's work. What God did on this day is in perfect agreement with the "third day" mentioned in 1 Corinthians 15.4, for the number "three" in the Scriptures always represents resurrection. The land now emerged from the waters. Formerly it had been buried beneath the darkness of the bitter seas; now it arose from its grave and became a dry land which could bear fruits. Though God did not eliminate the waters, He confined them to their limited boundaries. The seas now had their bounds; they could not deluge the land. God named the Seas (v.10) and thus recognized their existence. Not until the new heavens and the new earth arrive will the seas be eliminated. The dry land too was given a name—the name of Earth (v.10)—to distinguish it from the seas. This was the work of the first half of the third day. (The work on the third day was divided into two halves; on that day God spoke twice and twice He called it good. During the first half of the day, the earth came out of the water; during the second half of the day, the earth produced grass, herbs, and fruitful trees.)

We have noticed how, spiritually speaking, the cross was at work on the preceding day. Naturally what is typified here on the third day is resurrection. The death and the resurrection of Christ give us new life. Just as He died for us, so He was also raised for us (Rom. 4.25). Even as we need His death, so we also need His resurrection (Rom. 5.10). The absence of either one of these will reduce the gospel to vanity. Through the death of the Lord Jesus we are delivered from all which belongs to Adam—that is to say, to the natural. By His resurrection we can enter into all which belongs to Christ—that is to say, to the supernatural. His death delivers us from the position and experience of a sinner in order that we may no longer be sinners. His resurrection makes us righteous, obtaining the position and experience of the righteous. "Wherefore if any man is in Christ, he is a new creature: the old things are passed away; behold, they are become new" (2 Cor. 5.17).

The redemptive plan of God is not meant to repair or mend the old we have; it is to "re-create" us. He discards the old. He uses the death of the Lord Jesus to deliver us from the old, and He uses the resurrection of the Lord Jesus to get us into the new. As we are raised with Christ, we experience union with Him. As we experience being "in Christ," we experience the "new creation." If we are dead with Christ, we must also be raised together with Him. Thus shall we experience the life of a new creature.

Whatever is in the "old creation"—whether it is the old life or its nature or its works—can never satisfy God's heart. "In Adam all die" (1 Cor. 15.22). In God's eyes, all that is in our old creation has the mark of "death" in it. These dead things are beyond repair. God wants only that which is totally new. He wants "a new creature: the old things are passed away; behold, they are become new." For this reason, His primary work is the new birth, by which He gives a "new spirit and new heart" to man (this, as we showed earlier, is the work of the first day). This new spirit now works with the Spirit of God in delivering the old life with its nature to the cross (and this, as seen earlier, is the work of the second day). Having solved the problem of the "old things" God now begins to develop the "new creature" in His making all things new. Step by step He shall work until He has transformed even our body (this, by way of anticipation, is to be the work of the sixth day). We shall be totally new. This we shall touch upon later in our discussion.

The experience of resurrection (the third day) comes after that of regeneration (the first day) and that of co-death with Christ (the second day). Regeneration is the beginning of life. With a regenerated life, we are willing to co-operate with the Holy Spirit in our being crucified with Christ. And co-death with

Christ spontaneously leads to co-resurrection with
Him. "For if we have become united with him in the
likeness of his death, we shall be also in the likeness of
his resurrection" (Rom. 6.5). Regeneration gives us
life; resurrection gives us life more abundant. Were a
believer to stop at regeneration, he would not be able
to overcome sin. If he were to remain at the stage of
co-death, he would have no power to practice righteousness (that is, the holiness of God). So we need to
advance in our experiencing of Christ. Let us see that
we are regenerated first, then we are co-crucified, and
finally we are co-resurrected. In actual fact, however,
whenever we believe in the Lord Jesus and thus are
born again, at that very instant God has reckoned us
as having already been resurrected, though we may
have as yet to experience it in our life.

A great danger to many believers is this, that when
one looks within and fails to see that "the old things
are passed away: behold, they are become new," he
tends to think he is not yet born again or that such a
scriptural word is beyond human experience. Some
try their best to replenish their life so as to bring it up
to God's standard. But in actual experience they end
up in defeat, they having no peace or joy and losing
whatever liberty and power they profess to possess. If
only they would deny themselves and with faith look
up to Christ, they would experience victory. The
cause of much of our defeat lies in our desiring the
fruit of resurrection while rejecting the deep rooting
of co-crucifixion. Instead of letting the cross do a
deeper work in us, we are anxious to proceed to have
the resurrection life—thus unknowingly trying to

make new life out of the old one, which is an impossible task. For resurrection has its foundation in the cross. Without the cross, there can be no resurrection. Whoever wishes to experience resurrection must first experience the cross.

As regards our acceptance by God, it is not based on our subjective experiences. As we believe in the Lord Jesus, faith joins us to Christ. Our position of being "in Christ" causes us to be accepted by God automatically. God reckons us as being totally new. The acceptance in Christ is to be accepted *as* Christ. God looks not for our inward condition, He only sees our new position; and therefore He regards us as being totally new. This pertains to our objective salvation.

But there is also the other side. God wants us to be the body to His Son—which is to say, He wants us to experience all which our Head has accomplished for us. Thus shall we be delivered from the old creation and become the new creation ordained by God. We are raised together with Christ; we do not enter into resurrection by ourselves. Only by His resurrection do we come into this new realm, for we are resurrected with Him. By exercising our faith to accept this fact, we will be placed on dry land—free from the inundation of the old dark waters.

Just as the land came out of the waters, so shall our spirit come out in resurrection from the flesh. And even as the waters were not eliminated, so neither does the flesh become the spirit. Just as the waters were gathered together into one place and were not to cross its bounds, so the flesh, though still existing, shall be under our control through the death and resurrection of our Lord. The flesh is irredeemable and is wholly rejected by God. So then, all who died with Christ and have also been raised with Him belong to the flesh no more.

We have already seen the work of the first half of the third day. Now we shall see the work of the second half of this day. Having been raised, we will now bear fruit (vv.11,12). Fruit-bearing and resurrection are closely related. "Wherefore, my brethren, ye also were made dead to the law through the body of Christ; that ye should be joined to another, even to him who was raised from the dead, that we might bring forth fruit unto God" (Rom. 7.4)—"And being made free from sin, ye became servants of righteousness" (Rom. 6.18).

"And God called the dry land Earth." This word "earth" can also be translated as "soil." We know that soil can be broken up. If it is hard, it is not fertile. The smaller the lumps the soil is broken up into, the better it is for the harvest, because it may then supply nutrition to the planted seeds. Though the waters had subsided, the soil remained hardened and resisted the hand of the planter. In like manner, though the influence of the flesh may be lost, our natural life still clings to its "self-righteousness." It boasts of its natural ability and virtue, and it refuses to yield. But the broken soul life of a believer is like fertile soil in the hand of the heavenly Father. God asks not for our ability, He asks for our *in*ability. He does not require power from us but looks for weakness in us. He demands of us not to be full but to be empty. He expects not our resistance, instead He waits for our submission. He is the Almighty God, and His strength is manifested in our weakness. A broken field is the best ground for the growth of God's seed.

Fruit-bearing is not the result of keeping oneself intact; it is due to having oneself broken, made humble and weak, and casting oneself helplessly upon God. And thus does he allow God to work. Our own strength is an obstacle to the manifestation of God's power: "Except a grain of wheat fall into the earth and die, it abideth by itself alone; but if it die, it beareth much fruit" (John 12.24). Unless we hate our soul life with its natural ability, wisdom and virtue, we will not be able to bear much fruit. It is only after we cast aside the natural strength which comes from our flesh (just as the land which came out from the waters) and accept the hand of God with a broken heart that we are able to bear the fruit of God.

Often we reckon that only the sinful and unclean flesh must be destroyed; but we do not realize that denying our natural, good, correct, honest and righteous soul life is equally essential in this matter of fruit-bearing. We may have been content with our land, but God wants the soil of our heart to be broken. How highly do we look at ourselves! We fail to see that having been contaminated by sins this "I" of ours is weak and feeble! All of its good resolutions are like bubbles which vanish!

When we are weak in ourselves, being empty and bearing nothing but fully yielding as the clay to the potter's hand, the life of Christ shall begin to live in us and His power shall begin to be manifested through us. The more we know the reality of the cross and resurrection, the deeper we shall understand the real meaning of the breaking of the soul life.

This earth is not irrigated by the waters of the seas. Its productivity is not nurtured by the flesh. The mist (Gen. 2.6) is its nutrient: the Holy Spirit himself takes care of us. The ordinances of the flesh are "not of any value" (Col. 2.23) in fruit-bearing according to the truth. On the contrary, God limits the bounds of the flesh and calls it by its name (the flesh) to show that it can offer no help to the new creation but is itself condemned and irretrievable.

Even in fruit-bearing, there is progress. The grass comes first, then the herbs, and finally trees which bear fruit. Fruit is not for personal consumption, it is for the Lord: we are to "bring forth fruit unto God" (Rom. 7.4). All these fruits can propagate themselves: "Wherein is the seed thereof, after their kind" (Gen. 1.12). The kernel is each after its kind, and it is found in the fruit. Hence, love will reproduce love, joy will reproduce joy, and so on. Whenever we need love, we show forth love; whenever we need joy, we show forth joy. The fruit which is more exposed to the heat of the sun ripens earliest and is the most tasty. Man reaps what he has sown.

Seven

"And God said, Let there be lights in the firmament of heaven to divide the day from the night; and let them be for signs, and for seasons, and for days and years: and let them be for lights in the firmament of heaven to give light upon the earth: and it was so" (vv.14,15). The work this day is vastly different from the former work. The scene is now shifted from the earth to heaven. It is a work upon heaven, and it typifies the believer's ascension with Christ.

After resurrection, the sequential fact is ascension. For ascension is the indispensable truth following resurrection. Without ascension, our "new creation" will not be a complete work. Yet, as with the other truths such as our co-death and co-resurrection with Christ, ascension becomes factual and true to us as soon as we believe in the Lord Jesus because God has put us in this position of ascension. But our experience may still lag behind. We do not experience ascension until we have first experienced resurrection. If we are truly raised with Christ and joined to His resurrection life, we shall naturally bear fruit on earth and our spiritual life will ascend to heaven. God has "raised us up with him [Christ Jesus], and made us to sit with him in the heavenly places, in Christ Jesus" (Eph. 2.6). Ascension just naturally follows upon resurrection. Ascension life is what every saint must apprehend. After our Lord Jesus was risen from among the dead, He ascended to heaven where He is now seated at the right hand of God "far above all rule, and authority, and power, and dominion, and every name that is named" (Eph. 1.20,21). Ascension life is that life which overcomes all the powers of Satan. Formerly, we merely overcame the flesh, sin, and the world; now, in ascension, we are to experience the conflict and the victory over all powers and dominions, rulers and authority of darkness.

Once our spirit and soul are divided, and once our spirit due to resurrection is absolutely freed from the influence of soulish thought and emotion, we can be transcended so totally above all environments and worldly concerns that we are in possession of ascension life. Saints who have come into ascension life have the insight of the throne. They shall not be moved by anything. All who are truly crucified with Christ are truly raised with Christ; and all who are truly raised with Christ are truly ascended with Christ. "If then ye were raised together with Christ, seek the things that are above, where Christ is, seated on the right hand of God. Set your mind on the things that are above, not on the things that are upon the earth. For ye died, and your life is hid with Christ in God" (Col. 3.1–3).

Now the heavenly luminaries are divided into sun, moon and stars (v.16). The sun is the luminary of the day. It is the source of the heat and light for the earth. Its light is self-emitting, unchanging and constant. It is therefore a type of that real "heavenly Man." Though that heavenly Man, the Lord Jesus Christ, came to this world once, He has already returned into glory. Verse 2 of Malachi chapter 4 signifies to us that He is "the sun of righteousness." Our glorious Lord Jesus is the "greater light" in the heavenly places. While He was on earth, He was indeed "the day-spring [lit., (sun)rising] from on high" who "hath visited us" (Luke 1.78 mg.); He also was "the light of the world" (John 8.12). Although He was "the true light, even the light which lighteth every man, coming into the world" (John 1.9), yet "the light shineth in the darkness; and the darkness apprehended it not" (John 1.5). For in Jesus "the light [has] come into the world, [but] men loved the darkness rather than the light; for their works were evil. For every man that doeth evil hateth the light, and cometh not to the light, lest his works should be reproved" (John 3.19,20). Wherefore, the Lord Jesus returned to heaven where He is to dwell in the "tabernacle" (Ps. 19.4b) until the time of the millennial kingdom when He shall appear as "the sun of righteousness." Then "the sun" shall be "as a bridegroom coming out of his chamber, and rejoiceth as a strong man to run his course. His going forth is from the end of the heavens, and his circuit unto the ends of it; and there is nothing hid from the heat thereof" (Ps. 19.4-6).

Today His light does not lighten the world. Except for those who believe in Him, no one is under His en-lightenment: "And the world beholdeth me no more; but ye behold me" (John 14.19)—"But we behold him . . . even Jesus, . . . crowned with glory and honor" (Heb. 2.9)—"Wherefore he saith, Awake, thou that sleepest, and arise from the dead, and Christ shall shine upon thee" (Eph. 5.14).

In this current morally dark night of the world, men have lost the sense of the whereabouts of "the sun." Yet the church sees that sunlight, for she has ascended to heaven. Just as the moon reflects the light of the sun in the nighttime, so the church as she dwells in the light of Christ becomes the luminary in this dark night of the world that rejects Christ. On the first of the Six Days, we received the light. "Believe on the light, that ye may become sons of light" (John

12.36). So now, having "believed on the light," we are to reflect that light, we are to bear witness for Christ in this wicked generation: "Ye are the light of the world. . . . Even so let your light shine before men" (Matt. 5.14,16).

By being in this ascended position the saints can enjoy more intimate fellowship with the Lord. And as a result, will not the awful condition of this world's dark night be made more manifest and the power of darkness appear to be closer by? Will we not possess further insight and will not Christ become greater? What a position this is!

We know that the moonlight is second to the sunlight and far, far inferior to the latter. The moonlight serves as the light for the dark night; and in comparing it with its light source of the sun, it looks pale and silvery even at full moon. How it is subject to change, varying from full moon to crescent moon. The extent of the moon's light depends on the angle in which it is turned towards the sun. And sometimes it may even be totally eclipsed. Can we not see in this the spiritual meaning for us lesser lights who believe in "the sun of righteousness"? Alas, how changeable is the church! According to God's will, she is heavenly in nature and should always remain so. But according to human observation, she does not always stay that way. Oftentimes she seems to have completely disappeared. And even when she does stay heavenly, she rarely appears in fullness. Her turning away from her light source makes her abnormal. Is not her work to be one of constantly receiving light? For her light does not

originate in herself. She has no glory in herself, but all
the church's glory comes from her Lord. Only in His
light may she at all shine: "But we all, with unveiled
face beholding as in a mirror the glory of the Lord,
are transformed into the same image from glory to
glory, even as from the Lord the Spirit" (2 Cor. 3.18).
Just to be face to face with the Lord makes it a glorious day for her. Viewing from the earth, the church,
like the moon, really looks "fair" (Song of S. 6.10),
with "the precious things of the growth of the
moons" (Deut. 33.14). She "shall be established for
ever as the moon, and as the faithful witness in the
sky" (Ps. 89.37), and there shall be "abundance of
peace, till the moon be no more" (Ps. 72.7). Yet what
gives life to men is the direct ray of the sun. Our position in Christ as His body is indeed most precious,
and our experience of His warmth is most essential.
But when the sun comes out, the moon and the stars
disappear.

Whereas the moon typifies the church, stars today
are a type of individual saints. For they "are seen as
lights [Gk. *luminaries*] in the world" (Phil. 2.15). The
sun has gone and the moon shall soon pass away, and
so the stars shall appear on the scene: "they that are
wise shall shine as the brightness of the firmament;
and they that turn many to righteousness as the stars
for ever and ever" (Dan. 12.3).

God has created these stars that they may "rule"
(Gen. 1.16,17). Think of it, the light of the saints has
ruling power! How many sins must be concealed from
the saints. How many unclean things dare not come

near the believers. All who walk in the holiness, glory, righteousness, and the love of God have such ruling power.

Yet what the believers rule is the dark night. The greatest authority invested in the ascended Christians lies in their overcoming the power of darkness. Earlier in their walk, new believers were rather vague about spiritual warfare and lacked clear insight as to the wiles, assaults, temptations and counterfeits of the devil. But now, having come into an experience of their ascended position in heaven, they immediately begin to sense the actuality of the powers of darkness and today know how to overcome them by the blood of the Lamb and by the word of their testimony because they do not love their lives even to the extremity of death (Rev. 12.11).

They also know how to wield the sword of the Spirit—which is the word of God—in attacking the power of the enemy, as well as how to pray the challenging prayer of asking God to destroy all the works of the devil. They are learning how to stand on the solid foundation of the cross, how to keep to the victory already accomplished at Calvary, how to exercise their will to resist all the plots of the enemy, and how to use the words of praise to drive away the assaults of the evil spirits. Due to their ruling position, ascended believers will frequently have the experience of "bruis[ing] Satan under [their] feet" (Rom. 16.20).

Their light as stars in the firmament is to be used for "signs, and for seasons, and for days and years" as well as "to divide the light from the darkness" (Gen. 1.14,18). They know the signs of the times (cf.

Matt. 16.3). They understand how to discern the season because they have the insight of the throne. They clearly see through the affairs of the world and fully comprehend the phenomena of the last days. They are not disturbed by the rapid changes in the world scene when people are troubled and are at a loss as to what they should do, for they have a foreknowledge of these changes through their perceptive understanding of the Scriptures gained in the presence of God. In their ascended position, they are given knowledge as to what moves the Lord will make in these last days. They are aware of the attitude they should take towards the church as well as towards the world in the end time.

Ascended believers are ever conscious of the need of being watchful, for they know many false Christs and false prophets will arise to deceive the world (Matt. 24.24). Evil spirits as well as sinful angels will bring in confusion and entice the world—and even ignorant saints—to believe in Satanic doctrines and in strange and deceptive supernatural phenomena. Whoever does not have a firm foundation in God's word will surely be deceived. But having the insight of God, the ascended believers will not be cheated because they are not ignorant of the wiles of the devil. (2 Cor. 2.11)

Eight

"And God said, Let the waters swarm with swarms of living creatures, and let birds fly above the earth in the open firmament" (v.20). This is the work of the fifth day. Since this day stands between ascension and the Lord's second coming as King, its spiritual meaning is not hard to apprehend.

Here God *created* the fishes and the birds (see v.21), for the waters could not produce fishes by itself nor could the earth produce birds by itself. Both fishes and birds are created by God, who places them in the waters and on the earth. These fishes and birds are all living creatures (v.21), yet they possess different styles of living. As was mentioned before, the waters signify our sinful flesh whereby the latter causes us to enter into temptations; yet the grace of God succeeds in transforming us through it all. The earth coming out of the waters signifies the purified soul life. Once again, the goodness of God is able to form within us a new life-style.

Though our life has ascended to the heavenly place, we are nonetheless human beings in this world whose feet touch the earth. And hence we must manifest the life of God through our mortal flesh. Our ascended position in Christ in one sense causes us to leave the world; nevertheless, we today are still in the world. It is therefore incumbent upon us while still here on earth to express the life of God in our soul and body according to God's teaching.

Now quite obviously neither the waters nor the earth originally had any life in them, but God proceeded to create different life forms and to put them in those places. So that today the fishes in the waters manifest life there, and the birds in the air above the earth manifest life there. Even so, at the beginning of our Christian walk, there was originally no divine life in our flesh and soul. But upon entering into our ascended position in Christ in heaven through the new birth, the life of God will manifest itself in our daily walk—even in our flesh and soul. So that at this point, our life, like that of the fishes and the birds, seems to take upon itself a form. Yet despite the various degrees of outward form, the inward principle is one and the same—that of life. We ought to know, however, that this divine life is not inherent in the flesh or the soul, it only manifests itself in them. "That ye may become blameless and harmless, children of God without blemish in the midst of a crooked and perverse generation, among whom ye are seen as *lights* in the world, holding forth the word of *life*" (Phil. 2.15,16). On the one hand, "your life is hid with Christ in God" (Col 3.3)—this is ascension; on the other hand, you are to "put to death therefore your members which are upon the earth" (Col. 3.5)—this is the manifestation of life. And thus shall we be blessed by God (Gen 1.22).

Nine

"And God said, Let the earth bring forth living creatures after their kind, cattle, and creeping things, and beasts of the earth after their kind; and it was so" (v.24).

The work on the sixth day is like that of the third day, for it too is divided into two parts. The making of the living creatures on earth is the work done during the first part of the sixth day. This indicates that the outward expression of life is progressive. Here there is no water in view, and hence all that is spiritually represented here is the development of virtues in the new man.

It will be more meaningful if we look at the works of the fifth day and of the first part of the sixth day together. For all the fishes, birds, cattle, creeping things and beasts serve as types of men (see Matt. 4.19; Acts 10.12,28). Once a Christian begins to experience the ascension life, he becomes a channel for the life of God, channelling that life to many hearts. So that all these creatures have reference to our life and work now on earth.

Let us next look at the work of the latter part of the sixth day. "God created man in his own image" (vv.26,27). This brings us to the second coming of Christ, although in spiritual reality it is already a fact.

Having passed through the various spiritual stages of regeneration, co-crucifixion, co-resurrection, fruit-bearing ascension and manifestation of life, the saints progress naturally to become as perfect as God is perfect: "until Christ be formed in you" (Gal. 4.19) is the goal of spiritual life. It is only after we have experienced through union with Christ all these things which He has accomplished for us that we can arrive at being "transformed into the same image from glory to glory" (2 Cor. 3.18).

"Seeing that ye have put off the old man with his doings, and have put on the new man, that is being renewed unto knowledge after the image of him that created him" (Col 3.9,10)—"That ye put away, as concerning your former manner of life, the old man,

. . . and that ye be renewed in the spirit of your mind, and put on the new man, that after God hath been created in righteousness and holiness of truth" (Eph. 4.22–24). These passages underscore the fact that we should experience the perfectness of "the new man" in accordance with the life of God. "Put off," "put away" and "put on" are actions of the will. Believers need to exercise their will to reject all the works of the old man and to choose all the freshness of the new man. The apex of Christian living is the life of the will. With the will set, they shall be renewed in mind and knowledge according to the image of God. The mind is the battleground in spiritual warfare. It is *the* stronghold of the Adamic life as well as being that part of our life which is most corrupted by sin. If the mind be renewed, the image of God can easily be restored.

The *fullest* recovery to the image of God lies yet in the future—at the second coming of the Lord Jesus: "For our citizenship is in heaven; whence also we wait for a Saviour, the Lord Jesus Christ: who shall fashion anew the body of our humiliation; that it may be conformed to the body of His glory, according to the working whereby he is able even to subject all things unto himself" (Phil. 3.20,21)—"If he [Christ] shall be manifested, we shall be like him" (1 John 3.2).

The saints shall not only gain the image of God, they shall also have dominion over all things (vv.26,28). This brings us in our discussion to the millennial kingdom. At that time the saints shall rule and "reign with Christ a thousand years" (Rev. 20.4). Some of the saints shall even have "authority over ten cities" (Luke 19.17) in the kingdom!

Let us clearly understand that the glory of the millennial kingdom is not the automatic portion of all believers. It is only reserved for those who have experienced all the various spiritual stages of life as typified for us in Genesis 1. Those who are united with Christ in all His past experience shall also be united with Him in all His future glory. To be *saved* merely requires a person to believe in the Lord Jesus. But to *reign* with Christ demands faithfulness, suffering, and victory. The cross is the way to the crown; suffering is the condition for glory. God gives His gift of salvation freely to all, but He will not dispense His reward *gratis.* All who are willing for the Lord's sake to suffer loss in this world shall gain in the age to come. How could they receive glory in the next age if they have already reigned and gained in this life? Self-humbling is not an easy task, but can future exaltation and glory be something common? A holy life and faithful service cannot go unnoticed by the Lord.

Yet this millennial dominion of which the Bible speaks does not begin in the future. Actually we may "reign in life" now (Rom. 5.17), even though the full realization does await the future. Today we may indeed rule over all things by exercising the authority which our Lord has given to us. We should be kings today who rule over all the evil spirits by stopping their works. If Satan will eventually be bound during the millennial kingdom, we can certainly use "the powers of the age to come" (Heb. 6.5) *now* to confine his activities. We may also use today the weapon of prayer to control our circumstances. Whether it is a national, family, church or personal affair, we may govern it by prayer. We may even gain full self-control if we exercise our will to co-operate with the power of the Holy Spirit. This truly is victorious life. Christians in the millennial kingdom are most powerful.

Please note also that besides ruling as kings, the saints have their special food (Gen. 1.29): "And God said, Behold, I have given you every herb yielding seed, which is upon the face of all the earth, and every tree, in which is the fruit of a tree yielding seed; to you it shall be for food." A plant which yields seed is symbolic of life. It has the power of life within. Only that which has life in it is worthy to be our food. Do be aware that our food is part of our reward in the future: "To him that overcometh, to him will I give to eat of the tree of life, which is in the Paradise of God"—"To him that overcometh, to him will I give of the hidden manna" (Rev. 2.7,17). The matter of food continues after resurrection, for take note of the fact that after His resurrection our Lord still ate and drank with His disciples. In eternity in the heavenly city there will be the tree of life as food for us.

Today we are to foretaste what we shall have in the future. That which we eat gives us health, and living food nourishes the eater: "Man shall not live by bread alone, but by every word that proceedeth out of the mouth of God" (Matt. 4.4)—"My meat is to do the will of him that sent me, and to accomplish his work" (John 4.34)—"I am the bread of life" (John

6.35)—"He that eateth my flesh and drinketh my blood hath eternal life" (John 6.54). Today if we wish to be strong, we must feed upon God's word and upon the Lord Jesus. We must take God's will as our food. We cannot afford to read the Bible casually; instead, we need to digest the word of God by prayer and meditation so that our spiritual life may be nourished. Each time we faithfully do God's will, our inner man is once more nurtured. And each time when we by faith take into our life the death (Christ's flesh) and the life (Christ's words) of our Lord Jesus, we are given strength to march on. All who desire to be spiritually strong need to consume living food; all other is but chaff.

Ten

"And he rested on the seventh day from all his work which he had made" (2.2). The heavens and the earth and all the hosts of them therein that were created or made were finished. Spiritually speaking, God's work of redemption is done; so now there is nothing left but rest.

In the first chapter of Genesis God spoke more than ten times. All that He had spoken had eventually been accomplished. At every stage there was the working of God's word. All His works were but the outgrowth and development of His original latent power. In releasing His power step by step, God accomplished the plan He had first conceived. "For we are his workmanship, created in Christ Jesus" (Eph. 2.10). Blessed are they that obey the word of

God! Seven times God had said "good"; on the last occasion He said it was "very good." And why? Because He was now satisfied with His patient and delicate work. He rested because He was satisfied. This being *God's* rest, it quite logically brings us to the time of *eternal* rest in the new heaven and the new earth. It is then that we shall "enter into that rest [of God's]" (Heb. 4.3) and we shall ourselves have also "rested from [our] works, [even] as God did from his" (Heb. 4.10). Here eternity commences, and throughout the endless days we shall forever rest in God, know His will, marvel at His mercy, and praise His grace. What a glorious state! "Things which eye saw not, and ear heard not, and which entered not into the heart of man, whatsoever things God prepared for them that love him" (1 Cor. 2.9).

Yet thanks and praise be to God, we do not need to wait for the future to have this rest, for even today we may foretaste it: "Come unto me, all ye that labor and are heavy laden, and I will give you rest. Take my yoke upon you, and learn of me; for I am meek and lowly in heart: and ye shall find rest unto your souls" (Matt. 11.28,29). Here are two rests: the first one is given when we believe in the Lord Jesus as Savior; the second one is experienced after we learn of Christ. Our soul is bombarded with many lusts, excitements, desires, frustrations, distresses and sorrows; but we shall not grow weary and become faint if we consider the meekness and lowliness of our Lord who sets an example before us as the Lamb that bears the yoke and endures the contradiction of sinners. As we learn of Him we shall find rest in our soul. What a tranquil life! What a peaceful life! How happy we can be if we take God's will as the perfect life!

All Six Days were characterized by both "evening" and "morning." After each evening there was the morning. But on the seventh day—on God's sabbath day—there was neither evening nor morning. For what we now have is that which is perfect, complete and glorious. It is an endless day, blessed and sanctified by God.

Physical creation, we have seen, can serve as a type of spiritual creation. So that these ten stages in the history of the physical creation can represent what the believers will experience now and in the future: "Christ also loved the church, and gave himself up for it; that he might sanctify it, having cleansed it by the washing of water with the word, that he might present the church to himself a glorious church, not having spot or wrinkle or any such thing; but that it should be holy and without blemish" (Eph. 5.25–27).

How simple and plain is this that we have presented here. All who desire to know such teaching may understand the voice of creation which speaks to us in this way. For even the work in God's hand bears witness to His deep thought and great love. Creation and redemption are God's twofold work. They proclaim God himself in speechless acts and testify of Christ who is the key to the entire body of Scripture. We have not tried to falsify God's word to make it fit our own concept. For the word of God is ordained by God himself to bear witness to Him and to His Christ. And this is what we have tried to present.

5 | Creation and the Acts of Christ

Christ is the key to all truths. Without Him the Bible would be a dead book. Without Him we would never understand the Scriptures. When we are confronted with difficult passages in God's word, we will receive marvelous light if we can relate them to Christ. For the Bible centers upon just one person, without whom we could not know what it is speaking about. This one person is the Lord Jesus Christ. He himself declares: "Ye search the scriptures, . . . and these are they which bear witness of *me*" (John 5.39). This is likewise confirmed by these words of the Lord: "In the roll of the book it is written of *me*" (Heb. 10.7). The Bible is the written word of God, and Christ is the living Word of God. The written Word bears witness to the living Word, while the living Word fulfills the written Word. Just as we read of Christ in the Gospel according to Matthew, so we read of Him in the book of Genesis.

In our preceding discussion we saw how the physical creation is but a type of the spiritual one. Now we will see how the stages which God took in the physical creation are similar to the acts of Christ in the spiritual creation. As a matter of fact, that which God did in relation to the physical creation was also done by the Lord Jesus, since "all things were made through him [Christ the living Word]; and without him was not anything made that hath been made" (John 1.3)—"for in him were all things created" (Col. 1.16). Hence we shall see how much the works of Christ in the two creations are alike. May we be delivered from all our suppositions and be enabled by God's grace to perceive Christ according to the Scriptures. Since the physical creation is meant to be a type of the spiritual, it behooves us to see the similarity between these two creations in the hand of Christ.

The Need for Redemption

"In the beginning God created the heavens and the earth" (Gen. 1.1). Whatever God does is perfect. Nothing that passes through the hand of the Almighty can be tainted with sin or wrinkle or any such thing. That which He does is as beautiful and perfect as He himself is. How fresh and glorious are the things which come out newly from the hand of the Creator of the universe, the sole Potter! And such was the original condition of man, for God looked at him and pronounced it as being "very good."

Yet we know that such a good situation did not last long. For as soon as we read of the perfect heavens and earth having been created by God, we are instantly informed of the tragic story of its ruin. "[But] the earth [became] waste and void" (v.2a). What a difference between what is recorded in the first verse and what is announced in the second. The earth which God had created had changed! In between the events of these two verses there must have occurred a strange upheaval; otherwise, how could this beautiful earth have turned into waste and void? The Archangel had fallen! Sin had come in! This part of history is so painful that God was unwilling to narrate it plainly.

"And darkness was upon the face of the deep" (v.2b). This is a true picture of fallen mankind. Just as darkness covered the face of the deep, so spiritual and moral darkness in mind as well as in action prevails over all mankind born of the flesh. Darkness—it being the power of Satan—thus enslaves all men. No matter how men in "the deep" boast of their invention, manufacture, culture and knowledge, Satan has covered the deep with darkness so that no light of God will shine upon it. Yet men still boast of their unprecedented achievements in the twentieth century, not realizing they are under the power of Satan.

In such a situation men naturally speaking could have no hope of salvation. For God owed mankind no debt nor had He made any commitment to men that He must send His Son to save the world. Had He judged the world and condemned all men to eternal perdition, He would still have been just and righteous. Yet so infinite and immense was His royal grace that it far surpassed any human expectation. God planned the salvation of the world. And just as

He had restored the physical creation in six days, so He now redeems sinful men and accomplishes His spiritual creation through the redemption of Christ Jesus. We will now meditate on these steps which He has taken. How glad we are that we may speak more of Christ and think more of Him! May we worship and adore Him in silence as we contemplate the wonderful Savior and His wonderful salvation.

(1) The First Day's Work Signifies the Birth of the Lord Jesus

On the first day God brought in light and let it shine upon the darkness. Previously the deep had been blanketed with darkness, but now the light has come. Such was the first contact ever made between light and darkness. The world had never experienced such an incident before. This was the first time the light of the world had come to this dark world. Clearly this typifies the birth of the Lord Jesus. In speaking of the birth of the Lord Jesus and how the Word had become flesh, John proclaimed this: "And the light shineth in the darkness; and the darkness apprehended it not" (John 1.5). He also added: "There was the true light, even the light which lighteth every man, coming into the world" (John 1.9). John definitely viewed the birth of the Lord Jesus as light shining into our dark world. When Zacharias spoke of the birth of Christ, he too declared, "Because of the tender mercy of our God, . . . the *dayspring* [lit., *(sun)rising] from on high* hath *visited* us, to shine upon them that sit in darkness" (Luke 1.78,79 mg.).

Even our Lord Jesus himself acknowledged His birth in terms of light enlightening the world: "For God sent not the Son into the world to judge the world, but . . . that the light is come into the world" (John 3.17,19). These few scriptural passages which we have quoted are sufficient to prove that the work of God on the first day—light shining into darkness—is a type of how later on the Lord Jesus came into the world as the true light. The light has indeed come, yet the dark world is unwilling to be fully enlightened.

The first day's work constitutes the first step in the work of redemption. If light does not come to the world, there will be no point of contact between God and men. If the Lord Jesus does not come to this world, sinners will never see the Father as declared by the Only Begotten Son. Let us notice how parallel the first day's work is with the birth of the Lord Jesus.

The shining of the light is the work of the Holy Spirit. "And the Spirit of God *moved* [or, was brooding] upon the face of the waters" (v.2). But so was the incarnation the Holy Spirit's work: "And the angel answered and said unto her [Mary], The Holy Spirit shall come upon thee, and the power of the Most High shall *overshadow* thee: wherefore also the holy thing which is begotten shall be called the Son of God" (Luke 1.35). The Son of the Most High was born of the Holy Spirit, and yet men do not want to be born again of the Holy Spirit. On the first day, God called for light. "And God said, Let there be light: and there was light" (v.3). This fact (that of the Lord Jesus coming to the world to be light) we have already touched upon. Let us look at another passage of Scripture. When Simeon saw the child Jesus he blessed God and said: "Now lettest thou thy servant depart, Lord, according to thy word, in peace; for mine eyes have seen thy salvation, which thou hast prepared before the face of all peoples; a *light* for revelation to the Gentiles, and the glory of thy people Israel" (Luke 2.29–32). Who is truly open to be enlightened by Him?

"And God saw the light, that it was good" (v.4a). The first word spoken by God to our Lord Jesus was: "This is my beloved Son, in whom I am well pleased" (Matt. 3.17). Except for His own Son, no one can please the heart of the Father: for "they that are in the flesh cannot please God" (Rom. 8.8). One of the strange phenomena of sinful man is to assume that his own deeds are fully satisfying to God while the life of the Lord Jesus is in no way superior to his own! How blind is the natural man! He fails to see the beauty of Christ and to love Him. Yet God reckons this light to be good. Blessed is he who has the insight of God!

Light and darkness are now separated: "And God divided the light from the darkness" (v.4b). How much in harmony is this statement with what the Letter to the Hebrews says about the Lord Jesus: "For such a high priest became us, holy, guileless, undefiled, *separated* from sinners, and made higher than the heavens" (7.26). How very different is this Son of man from the ordinary sons of man! Though He is willing to take part in flesh and blood, He does not share in man's sinful nature. As light is distinguished from darkness, so Christ is different from sinful man. God gave light a name: "And God called the light

Day" (v.5a). Similarly, God gave Christ a name. The name of Jesus was not given Him by Joseph and Mary. Even when He was in His mother's womb, the angel told Joseph: "And she [Mary] shall bring forth a son; and thou shalt call his name Jesus; for it is he that shall save his people from their sins" (Matt. 1.21). Long before He was ever born, it was being prophesied that "from the bowels of my mother hath he [Jehovah] made mention of my name" (Is. 49.1). He is Jesus, therefore He is Savior. Now that the Savior has come, how do you treat Him? The world had not asked for a Savior, yet He in grace came into this world. The Savior has come, the Light has shone, but who among men will receive Him?

What is man basically like? He is very feeble and is but dust. He is limited and finite. If he has any virtue, that virtue is rather circumscribed. His thought, his character, his conduct and morality are restricted to the human plane. There is absolutely no way for him to rise higher. The common characterization of man is weak, fallen and sinful. Though he may have one or two strong points, he cannot transcend the boundary of man. If this is what man is basically like, then how can God ever be satisfied with him? For God is perfect, and He demands perfection. Unless man's character, morality, conduct and thought can match God's standard of righteousness, he can never be God's companion and abide with Him in heaven. Hence if man cannot make himself perfect as God is perfect, he cannot be saved. Who, then, among men has any hope?

It is for this reason that incarnation is the first act

of salvation. It is most essential for God to become man. The birth of the Lord Jesus is the union of divinity with humanity. The Lord Jesus is God, yet He became man. He therefore is God and yet man, man and yet God. In the past there had existed a great gulf between God and man. God could never be changed to man and man could never be changed to God. But now the Lord Jesus has come into this world. He is the Word that is become flesh. He is the bridge connecting God and man. For both God and man meet in Him. Man does not change to God nor does God change to man; yet in being perfect God and perfect man in His person, the Lord Jesus can manifest God as well as represent man. And because He is both God and man in perfect union, through Him our Father God can show grace to men. Because He is man as well as God, men can draw near to God in Him. Now that there is a true man on earth—a real man who is full of divine nature—it is possible for men to receive the life of God. And since God and man are joined in the Lord Jesus, this makes possible the union of God and men hereafter. Incarnation is not the whole story of the gospel; it is but the first move in the way of salvation. Nevertheless, this move does proclaim the nature and consequence of the coming salvation.

There are other reasons, however, for incarnation. The Son of God took part in flesh and blood in order that He (1) "might bring to nought him that had the power of death, that is, the devil"; and (2) "might deliver all them who through fear of death were all their lifetime subject to bondage" (Heb. 2.14,15). Men have sinned; and the wages of sin is death. He who has the power of death is the devil. Sin brings men to death and the devil rules over men through death. Hence in saving men, God must (1) solve the problem of the penalty of sin, and (2) solve the problem of the power of death held by the devil. The penalty of sin is death. He who has no flesh and blood cannot die; therefore the Lord Jesus must take upon himself flesh and blood. And once having a body, He could then die to atone for the sins of the world. For this reason the Scriptures say this: "a body didst thou [God] prepare for me"—"Lo, I am come . . . to do thy will, O God"—and this will is "the offering of the body of Jesus Christ once for all. . . . he [having] offered one sacrifice for sins for ever" (Heb. 10.5,7,10,12). The devil holds the power of death because no one can overcome death. But now the Lord Jesus has died and been resurrected in the human body, thus overcoming whatever power the devil may possess, even destroying the devil himself.

Since men have sinned, they must die. God cannot forsake righteousness in order to dispense grace. He cannot save men without punishing sins. Although He wants to save men, He must also punish them for their sins. So God himself came into the world to become man and to receive in himself as a man the penalty of sins for men. And thus sin can be judged but men can be saved. Furthermore, it is *men* who sin, so it must be a *man* who receives the penalty of sin. God *cannot* die; yet even if He could, He would die in vain; for it is men and not God who sin. This is another reason why God must become *man*. Mankind has sinned, therefore the "one mediator . . . between

God and men" must be "himself *man,* [even] Jesus
Christ" (1 Tim. 2.5). Christ is the unique man, in that
He included all mankind in himself and received the
penalty of sin. This is in perfect accord with law. It is
most just. For if we suppose that the Lord Jesus is the
Lord Jesus and men are men, then the death of the
Lord Jesus cannot be reckoned as men receiving the
penalty of sin. Nevertheless, though He is God, He is
truly man. He is in such complete union with men
that His death is recognized as the death of all mankind. Because the Lord Jesus has no sin, He should
not die. Therefore, His death is substitutionary. And
this is what incarnation has accomplished.

On the other hand, Christ must also be *God;*
otherwise, redemption would not be fair. Because He
is God, He is the One whom the world has sinned
against. He therefore has the authority both to accept
the opposition and to forgive them. If Christ were not
God as well as man, He would merely be an innocent
third party and not the party being defrauded. To ask
an innocent bystander to die for the sinful would not
seem fair, although it would be most gracious. Yet
Christ is not a third party, He is instead directly involved. He is the One who is offended because He is
God. And consequently, He has the authority to
forgive as well as to endure the sufferings.

Incarnation is not the whole story of salvation, for
the finished work of redemption is ultimately
achieved on the cross. Even so, incarnation is the first
step taken. Without His emptying himself and taking
on the likeness of men, Christ could not die for men
and save them. Bethlehem is the harbinger of

Golgotha. Without Bethlehem there can be no Calvary. What amazing grace that the Son of God should sacrifice himself for men! What a glorious mystery that the Son of God should become flesh!

(2) The Second Day's Work Signifies
the Death of the Lord Jesus

In the work of the second day God made the firmament to divide the waters from the waters. This firmament is called heaven. Formerly all the waters were together, but now the firmament came to divide the waters which were under the firmament from the waters which were above the firmament. This heaven of air plainly typifies the cross of the Lord Jesus Christ because in the work of the second day, separation is the main theme.

This division came in two parts: the first part was to make a firmament in the midst of the waters; and the second part was to divide the waters above and below the firmament. Did not the cross of Christ make the same separations? Did not the Lord Jesus cry out as He was crucified, "My God, my God, why hast thou forsaken me?" (Matt. 27.46) He was thus separated from God. And the Scriptures further record that "he was cut off out of the land of the living" (Is. 53.8). This speaks of how He was separated from men.

The work on the second day is the most important part of the work of redemption. For without the shedding of blood there can be no remission of sin. What the world lacks is not a brilliant model. Light is good, but it only exposes the true condition of men's corruption and fall. And hence, the greater the light, the deeper the condemnation. Without the redemptive work which came afterwards, the birth of Christ can only serve as the strongest evidence for the condemnation of the world; for if there is at least one human being who can live such a holy and righteous life, why can not all men live likewise? If one person can, it means all may and should. Since one man can and does what all the rest do not, this silences the possibility of there being any excuses for not doing so. If the Lord Jesus had come into this world and done nothing else, His life would no doubt condemn the sins of the whole world. Therefore, if His birth had not been for the sake of redemption, it would have been better for Him not to have been born. For His thoughts, words, deeds and life-style are all beyond human achievement. And thus He would condemn men everywhere.

The veil which hangs before the holiest of all is beautiful and glorious, but it separates man from the holiest of all. It is this veil which bars people from entering the holiest place so as to appear before God. Hence only a *rent* veil opens up a living way to God. The Christ who only lives drives men away from God; but the Christ who is also torn and rent and who *dies* brings all sinners to the holiest of all: "Who [Christ] his own self bare our sins in his body upon the tree . . . Because Christ also suffered for sins once, the righteous for the unrighteous, that he might bring us to God" (1 Peter 2.24, 3.18). As long as He only lives, no man may draw nigh to God.

Now let us observe how the cross of the Lord
Jesus is comparable to the work done by God on the
second day. God did not make the firmament right
away. He first decided what to do, and then He did it.
Hence in verse 6 He said, "Let there be a firmament
in the midst of the waters"—this was God's pre-
determined plan. In verse 7, though, we read this:
"And God made the firmament"—this is the act of
God. Before the cross was ever set up on the hill of
Calvary, it had been pre-determined by God. The
later cross and the firmament here have tremendous
resemblance to each other. The death of the Lord
Jesus was not accidental, it was something pre-
determined. Christ "was foreknown indeed before
the foundation of the world, but was manifested at
the end of the times for your sake" (1 Peter 1.20). He
is "the Lamb that hath been slain from the foundation of the world" (Rev. 13.9 mg.). So that the death
of the Lord Jesus resembles the work of the second
day in that it was pre-determined before it was actually carried out.

This firmament was put in *the midst* of the waters.
Waters in the Scriptures represent peoples: "He saith
unto me, The waters which thou sawest . . . are
peoples, and multitudes, and nations, and tongues"
(Rev. 17.15). Like the firmament, the cross stands in
the midst of the peoples and is lifted up for the sake
of men: "Where they crucified him, and with him
two others, on either side one, and Jesus in the
midst" (John 19.18). Actually, the hill of Calvary
may be considered the focal point of the world. Christ
died in the midst of men and for the sake of men.

As we have read before, this firmament also *divided* the waters. So does the cross of our Lord Jesus divide the world of men. When He was crucified, His cross divided the two robbers eternally. One went to Paradise, the other descended to Hades. In their past life they had sinned with one accord; but now at the last moments of their earthly life, one received the substitutionary death of the Lord Jesus but the other totally rejected Him. And thus these two men's fate underscored the distinction between heaven and hell. It was an eternal separation. And just as the cross of Christ has separated these two robbers, so it continues even now to divide the entire world. From the distant past to the immediate present, His cross has continued to separate the world into two classes: the saved and the perishing: "For the word of the cross is to them that *perish* foolishness; but unto us who are *saved* it is the power of God" (1 Cor. 1.18). The cross separates the saved from those who perish. Whether one is to be saved or to perish does not depend upon the person but on how that one treats the cross. The firmament of old had alone divided the waters above and beneath it; even so, the cross today uniquely separates the saved from the perishing.

This firmament in the midst so divided the gathered waters that the waters which came to be located above the firmament did not fall down. The firmament supported the waters above it in such a way that they would not descend and mix in with the waters beneath lest they again returned to the condition of waste and void that had been God's judgment.

We have already seen from Revelation 17 that

waters represent the peoples. The waters above, though, have a different meaning. During the days of Noah, God had endured the sins of men long enough and had decided to punish them. He opened the windows of heaven and poured down the waters from above. And thus we can conclude from this that the waters above represent the wrath, the punishment, the judgment of God.

By inference we may then discover the meaning of the firmament. It upholds the waters above so that they may not fall down to the waters beneath. It stands between the waters above and the waters beneath. And this is precisely what the work of the cross is. The Lord Jesus was crucified that He might bear our sins. In this sense He is our covering. The judgment, punishment and wrath of God should come upon us and cause us to be as desolate as "the deep"; yet the Lord Jesus placed himself between God's wrath and us. For as He was being crucified, Christ Jesus allowed the wrath of God to fall on himself instead of it falling upon us. God's wrath *should* fall on us (see John 3.36), but God has set Christ up as our substitute whereby "Jehovah hath laid on him [Christ] the iniquity of us all" (Is. 53.6).

Thank God for the airy heaven which divides the waters above and beneath! Thank God for the cross of the Lord Jesus which separates and shields the wrath of God from men! Thank God that Christ was willing to receive what we ought to have received —even God's wrath! Now this is salvation. And this is the gospel. If the waters above and beneath had not been divided, the world would forever have sunk beneath the waters. Without the substitutionary death of the Lord Jesus, men would have remained under the wrath of God—in waste and void—with no remedy whatsoever. This is therefore the substitutionary work of the cross.

The firmament was made by God. It was He who both prepared and performed. Outwardly, the Lord Jesus was crucified by the Jews and the Gentiles—as though it were men who took away His life. But according to the Scriptures, in actuality He was not killed by men since He himself declared that no one could take His life away from Him (see John 10.18). He died because God judged in Him the sins of the world: "Yet it pleased Jehovah to bruise him; he hath put him to grief: when thou shalt make his soul an offering for sin . . ." (Is. 53.10). So that the event of the cross was a direct act of God and not merely the result of the ill-treatment meted out to Christ by men: "Him being delivered up by the determinate counsel and foreknowledge of God, ye by the hand of lawless men did crucify and slay" (Acts 2.23).

We will recall that of the Six Days' work done by God, only concerning the work of this second day (involving the firmament) did He not say that what He had made was good. What God does not say carries equal weight to what He does say. In this second day's work, God dealt with sin by the cross. His wrath was poured out upon the righteous One so that the unrighteous might be set free. Here God made the sinless One to be sin for us and allowed Him to receive the penalty for us all. Is it not therefore full of meaning that God did not declare that it was "good" here? He takes no delight in punishing sin. He loves instead to show grace; in no way does He like to condemn.

The redemption of the cross is the basis of salvation. Without the subsequent substitutionary death of the cross, the birth of our Lord Jesus would of itself be of no help. For all have sinned and the wages of sin is death. So that unless there is a Savior who would die in our stead, sinners could not escape the penalty they deserve. The birth of Christ alone will not solve the problem confronting sinners. What men need is a Savior who is willing to bear our sins, not just a holy teacher. Only a Savior who dies for us can deliver us from our sins. For how can there be any resurrection if there be no death? Resurrection under those circumstances would not be needed. Hence all the realities of salvation are based on this second day's work. Without the dividing of the waters, the land could not appear later nor would the light of the first day shine for any positive purpose. Let us therefore pay special attention to what this second day's work points towards —even the substitutionary death of the Lord Jesus on the cross.

(3) The Third Day's Work Signifies the Resurrection of the Lord Jesus

On the third day, God commanded (1) that the waters under the heavens be gathered together into one place so as to let the dry land appear, and (2) that the earth put forth grass, herbs yielding seed, and fruit trees bearing fruit. Formerly the land had been covered by the waters of the deep. It had no life nor activity. For the land was deeply buried beneath the waters of the judgment of God. Except for the darkness there was nothing else—apart from the rolling of angry waves there was no sight of any land. And with the land thus deeply buried, how could there be any life? But now, God began to work. First, He called for the land to emerge out from beneath the waters; then He caused life to reappear upon the earth. So that this third day's work typifies the resurrection of the Lord Jesus.

"A third day" (v.13)—this is sufficient to prove that this day's work does indeed typify resurrection: "He hath been raised on the third day" (1 Cor. 15.4). In the Bible we may find many passages wherein the third day and resurrection are joined together. This occurs not only in the New Testament, it also occurs in the Old. For example, the third day after Passover is the Feast of the First Fruits. This unquestionably speaks to us of the resurrection of Christ (our Paschal Lamb) on the third day after He died. As we read what Paul said in 1 Corinthians 15 we ought to notice a rather special phrase of his: "He hath been raised on the third day *according to the scriptures*" (v.4). By this statement we can know that the resurrection of the Lord Jesus on the third day had been prophesied already in the Old Testament—the latter being the Scriptures in Paul's day. Now we will not have time to look at every passage where this "third day" has been written in the Scriptures, but we ought to at least look into Genesis 1.13 where the "third day" was first mentioned. Let us see how this third day of God's work typified the resurrection of the Lord Jesus.

Not just the number three (as in the "third day") is significant, the *work done* on the third day also bears witness to the resurrection. The land was previously buried under the waters. Now, though, "the dry land appears" (v.9). Once it was under the waters, now it shall rise above the waters. Is not this resurrection? The land which once was covered by waters reappeared as from a watery tomb. It arose above the waters and remained higher than the waters. What a beautiful picture of resurrection! We may appreciate this picture in Christian water baptism, for when a person is baptized, his whole body is first immersed in water and then he comes up out of the water. Both Romans 6.4 and Colossians 2.12 tell us that this baptism is a type of death, burial and resurrection. The land appearing out of the waters therefore serves as a type of resurrection out of death and burial.

Isaiah 57.20 tells us how water symbolizes *wickedness:* "the wicked are like the troubled sea; for it cannot rest, and its waters cast up mire and dirt." The land was buried in the waters just as the Lord Jesus was buried in the tomb. Yet the land did not remain forever under the waters because it appeared out of the waters on the third day. This too can be likened to the resurrection of the Lord Jesus. Romans 6.6–11 presents this matter most clearly in showing the relationship between the resurrection of the Lord Jesus and *sin:* "knowing that Christ being raised from the dead dieth no more; death no more hath dominion over him. For the death that he died, he died unto sin once: but the life that he liveth, he liveth unto God" (vv.9,10). Just as the land appeared out of the waters, so Christ was raised from the dead and apart from sin.

The work of the third day had a second part: new life sprang forth upon the earth. This like the first part of the day's work also speaks of resurrection: "And the earth brought forth grass, herbs yielding seed after their kind, and trees bearing fruit . . . after their kind" (v.12). Before this occurred there was no life on the judged earth, but now life appeared. Formerly death reigned, but now life had come. God did not call forth life on the second day nor on the fourth day but on resurrection day, *the third day:* "We were buried therefore with him through baptism into death: that like as Christ was raised from the dead through the glory of the Father, so we also might walk in *newness of life"* (Rom. 6.4). Before resurrection, there was no new life. For new life can only come after resurrection. Before the land appeared out of the waters, no living things could grow. But once there is a coming up out of the water, things can grow. First resurrection, then life. After resurrection, there must be new life; otherwise, resurrection accomplishes nothing. All who desire spiritual growth should take note of this.

In this second stage of the third day's work, special emphasis is laid on fruit. For this is the natural result of resurrection. The very purpose of resurrection is to bear fruit. Else what use would there be for the land to appear out of the waters? The land reappeared in order to bear fruit. The Bible is not at all silent on the relationship between resurrection and fruit-bearing: "But now being made free from sin and become servants to God, ye have your *fruit* unto sanctification, and the end eternal life" (Rom. 6.22). How are we made free from sin? Through co-death, co-burial, and co-resurrection with the Lord. What happens after resurrection? We see "fruit unto sanctification." Hence fruit-bearing is bound to come after resurrection: "Wherefore, my brethren, ye also were made dead to the law through the body of Christ; that ye should be joined to another, even to him who was raised from the dead, that we might bring forth *fruit* unto God" (Rom. 7.4). No death, no resurrection; no resurrection, no fruit. Bearing "fruit unto God" can come only through dying and being raised with the Lord Jesus. Any fruit that is recognized by God has its foundation only in the death and resurrection of the Lord Jesus. That which has not passed through death and resurrection belongs to the old creation. It is condemned by God and is not fit to be called fruit.

The work today is resurrection. Incarnation is important, crucifixion is equally important, but without resurrection there will not be the full gospel. Birth is for crucifixion, and the consequence of crucifixion is resurrection. Resurrection means that God has accepted the salvation which the Lord Jesus accomplished through His death: Christ "was delivered up for our trespasses, and was raised for our justification" (Rom. 4.25).

This verse from Romans indicates two things: (1) that the Lord Jesus died to bear our sins, and that through His death He received the penalty of our sins that we might be forgiven. Forgiveness of sins is the negative aspect of salvation, showing that though we have sinned, our sins are being forgiven by God. But (2) that His resurrection is for our justification. Justification is salvation's positive aspect, showing that we have no sin because God declares us to be without sin. Yet how can we be deemed to be without sin? This is because the negative work is done so thoroughly that all our sins are being forgiven and cleansed. On the basis of the death of the Lord Jesus and the forgiveness we have received, God justifies us. Yet this justification is given us through the resurrection of the Lord Jesus. His death has accomplished redemption, our sins are forgiven. And now on the ground of the resurrection of our Lord Jesus, God pronounces us as being without sin and He thus justifies us.

Resurrection causes us to have a new relationship with God. Due to the resurrection of the Lord Jesus, we now stand before God on a new basis and in a new position. Death and resurrection are closely joined; hence forgiveness and justification are tightly entwined. Jesus' resurrection indicates that God has accepted His death. Moreover, justification proves that we have been forgiven by God. Because of the death of the Lord Jesus, a Christian feels in his spirit that his sins have been borne away by the Lord, judged in Christ, and forgiven by God. This is negative. Because of the resurrection of the Lord Jesus, he senses in his spirit that he is no longer a forgiven miserable prisoner but a child of God fully accepted. Resurrection means that all in the past is dead. Whatever is of sin and of self has been buried in the tomb, out of sight and nevermore to be seen. What the Christian now has is altogether new.

Let us therefore not only be forgiven Christians who know that our sins are forgiven but let us also be justified Christians who live daily before God in the new position which the resurrection of the Lord Jesus has given us. We believe daily that we are accepted in Christ even as Christ is accepted by the Father. As God is pleased with Christ, so He is pleased with us, for we are joined to Christ in both His death and resurrection.

(4) The Fourth Day's Work Signifies the Ascension of the Lord Jesus

In the work of the fourth day, God made the lights (Gen. 1.14–18). He made sun, moon and stars. The work of yesterday (the third day) took place on earth; this day's work of God takes place in heaven. The attention is now focused on the things in heaven. For sun, moon and stars are all celestial bodies. On this fourth day God makes these lights for several purposes: (1) "to give light upon the earth" (v.17). Darkness is the typical nature of the world, but light is a special feature in the world. Ordinarily the world is pitch dark, so light must shine or else the world will remain in a long night. And (2) "to rule over the day and over the night, and to divide the light from the darkness" (v.18). Light is not only to shine but is also to rule. This day's work is a type of the ascension of the Lord Jesus.

All the works done on this day were executed in the firmament of heaven. It was not like the first day of God's work when light shone into the world. Though there were lights, yet they shone from heaven. The light that came into this world has now returned to heaven. And this is ascension. The Lord Jesus who came down from heaven has now been received back to heaven from earth (cf. Acts 3.21).

Malachi 4.2 tells us that Christ is the sun of righteousness. Both Revelation 12.1 and Psalm 19.5,6 support the same thought. The conclusion we draw from studying the Scriptures is that the sun is a type of Christ. We now see Him not in the world but *in heaven.* For our sake He has ascended back to heaven where He now appears before God to be our Advocate and High Priest.

This day's work speaks not only of Christ but also of His people. For the moon is a type of the church; and stars, a type of individual Christians. Through His death and resurrection the Lord has gathered a people to His name. So that we see here the moon and stars being mentioned with the sun. The moon has no light in itself; it merely reflects the light of the sun. In like manner, the church herself has no light, she merely reflects the light of Christ. Believers today are seen as lights in the world (Phil. 2.15), and thus are like the stars.

The work we must do as lights has two aspects to it: the first is to reflect the light of Christ in this morally dark night of the world, and the second is to rule over the powers of darkness by means of the light of our words and deeds. In the millennial kingdom we shall truly be kings and rule over all things.

The ascension of Christ concludes His earthly work. His ascension is based on His death and resurrection. It signifies the fact that He has overcome all which belongs to the Satanic kingdom. "He [God] raised him [Christ] from the dead, and made him to sit at his right hand in the heavenly places, far above all rule, and authority, and power, and dominion, and every name that is named, not only in this world, but also in that which is to come" (Eph. 1.20,21). We know that the rule, authority, power and dominion mentioned here refer to Satan and his servants. So that the meaning of the ascension of the Lord Jesus is that God has given Him a place higher than all the powers of Satan. His heavenly place is an overcoming position above Satan. The latter is now under His feet, with no further opportunity to attack Him; for He now is the Lord and Head over all things: "Wherefore also God highly exalted him, and gave unto him the name which is above every name; that in the name of Jesus every knee should bow, of things in heaven and things on earth and things under the earth, and that every tongue should confess that Jesus Christ is Lord, to the glory of God the Father" (Phil. 2.9-11).

In ascension, our Lord Jesus obtains the highest place, far beyond the touch of Satan and his evil spirits. Even they must confess that Jesus Christ is Lord and King. How important is this position, without which the impact and effect of the death and resurrection of our Lord Jesus upon earth would be affected by the evil forces. The Lord himself is now leading His own people to take this heavenly position with Him so that they may shine for Him on the one hand and overcome the powers of darkness which attack them on the other hand. This is told to us in Ephesians 2.6: "And [God] raised us up with him, and made us to sit with him in the heavenly places, in Christ Jesus." Just as the light of the sun overcomes darkness, so the heavenly position of Christ overcomes the powers of darkness. And just as the moon and stars dwell with the sun in heaven, so Christians abide with Christ in the heavenly places.

(5) The Fifth Day's Work Signifies Christ Jesus as the Lord of Life

In the work of the fifth day (Gen. 1.20-23), God created many living creatures of the seas and birds of the air. Actually, all the works of the preceding four days were but preparation in both the heaven and the earth to make them as proper habitations for these living creatures. Not until then did these living creatures appear in the air as well as in the waters. Though there were plants on the third day, there was no sign of any animals or birds. The living creatures of the waters could live in the waters only because God had prepared the waters. The living creatures of the air could fly in the air only because God had prepared the firmament. Both the fishes and the birds have life, though they have different bodily forms. In man's eye, the birds are quite different from the fishes in their diversity; yet the life these birds have is the same. Their difference is in the outer form, not in the life itself that animates them all. So we may say that the fifth day's work is the formation of life. Some living creatures were formed in the waters while others were formed in the air. Thus the fifth day's work is a type of the Lord Jesus as the life-giving Lord.

Life in itself is not self-existent. It is created by God. God is the Creator of all life. What is therefore suggested here is simply this—that Jesus Christ is the Lord of life. No matter what form life may take, the life itself comes from God. After the Lord was resurrected and ascended to heaven, His work thereafter was to give life to men that they might have it and have it more abundantly (John 10.10). His ascension, which is typified by the work of the previous day, is to be life to the saints. This may be seen in the Letter to the Colossians. First this passage: "If then ye were raised together with Christ, seek the things that are above, where Christ is, seated on the right hand of God" (3.1). This verse speaks of resurrection and ascension. And what follows is this passage: "Your life is hid with Christ in God. . . . Christ who is our life . . ." (3.3,4). Accordingly, the work of Christ after His ascension is that of being our very life in God.

We have already mentioned how birds and fishes may represent the people; now we will perceive how they may resemble the spiritual life of the Christians.

Life, we learned above, is given by the Lord Jesus. He has already ascended to heaven, and His purpose now is to cause His saints to express His life in a practical way before His return. Life without a body cannot exist on earth, nor can it experience anything. Without this body, life cannot be expressed. Hence "formation" is necessary to the expression of life. What the Lord desires of His saints today is that they may manifest in a practical way the life they receive through His death and resurrection. They have already received life through the death and resurrection of the Lord, and they have also obtained a heavenly position. What they lack now is to be so formed on earth as to *express* the Lord's life. This is the meaning and purpose for today's work by Christ.

The Lord Jesus is now disciplining His saints that they may take form. Just as the birds and the fishes express their life through their bodies, so the Lord wants His saints to have definite form in this world. He seems to call His own to express His life through their bodies wherever they may be located. The life is the same, though each believer has his or her individual body. Hence the *manifestation* of the inner life must also vary. All the saints receive the same life from the Lord Jesus. Yet due to the variety inherent in individuality these same saints exhibit the Lord's life differently. This truth we may see delineated in the parable of the sower (see Matt. 13). Although the seed sown is the same, and the life germinated from the seed is also the same, and even the field is the same, yet there are marked differences in the fruitful yields: some were thirtyfold, some were sixtyfold, and some a hundredfold. We receive from the Lord the same life, but due to the difference in the "form" or "outlet," life assumes different manifestations.

So in this fifth day's work, the Lord Jesus calls His saints to experiment on earth with His life that they may express it through their various individualities. This is very important. For unless the life which we receive through regeneration and through the death, resurrection and ascension of our Lord is being expressed experimentally on earth, we have not been deeply united with that life.

Life is deprived of expression if it has no body. Through the body of a bird the birdlife within can be given expression. It is therefore a kind of discipline for the saints that once receiving the life of the Lord they should manifest it practically on earth. What the birds and the fishes experience of life begins at the moment when their life takes up their bodies. Thereafter they may experience their different life-styles. This speaks of the discipline of the saints. The present work of the Lord Jesus is to discipline His saints in life. But obviously, there must be union with the life of the Lord before there can be any discipline.

(6) The Sixth Day's Work Signifies the Lord's Second Coming and His Being King

In the work of the sixth day, God created Adam in His own image and commissioned him to rule the earth (Gen 1.26–28). With the works of the preceding five days now done, everything on earth and in heaven was ready. Man's food and lodging were now all prepared. Hence God could create man. In this act of creation, the most important facet of it was the fact that man was created in God's image. For man was to represent God on earth. Man was to declare God. And this speaks to us of the second coming of the Lord Jesus.

The Lord Jesus is the last Adam as well as the second man. The first Adam is actually a type of the Lord Jesus. And because he was created in God's image, we can see in him a type of the Lord's second coming; for when He shall return, His body—that is to say, His church—shall be completed and shall be like Him: "If he [Christ] shall be manifested, we shall be *like* him" (1 John 3.2). At the time He appears again, His church shall be completely like Him. Just as the first Adam had been created in God's image, so the body of the last Adam—the church—shall be like God at the return of the Lord Jesus, for all the saints shall have His image and shall manifest Him in the glorious bodies which He shall give us.

On the sixth day as well, Eve was built to be Adam's wife (see Gen. 1.27, 2.21,22 mg.). Eve was meant to be a type of the church. At the return of the Lord Jesus, the church will be completed and offered to Christ as His bride. Together they shall rule the world. Eve was made on the sixth day. The completion of the church awaits the coming again of the Lord Jesus. At that time she shall be His bride. For these reasons, the work of the sixth day in creating Adam and Eve speaks plainly of the things concerning the Lord's second coming.

Not only did God create Adam and Eve, He also appointed them to rule over the world He had created

(Gen. 1.28). All powers were given to them. God did not rule the world directly; He delegated this authority to Adam. At the return of Christ to earth, He shall set up a millennial kingdom to rule the world. The first part of the sixth day's work (that of creating Adam) pertains to the Lord's second coming, and the second part of the sixth day's work (that of appointing Adam to rule the world) pertains to the Lord being King. In the millennial kingdom, God shall give all authority to Christ and let Him reign: "Wherefore also God highly exalted him, and gave unto him the name which is above every name" (Phil. 2.9). There are many passages in the Bible which refer to God giving authority to Christ that He might be the Lord of all in the millennial kingdom.

Adam shared his authority with Eve. Although it was Adam who directly ruled the world, Eve helped him in ruling. The Bible frequently mentions how Christians—who are to be the Eve of the Lord Jesus—shall reign with Christ and share in His glory when He becomes King in the millennial kingdom. Even as Christ rules over all things, so Christians shall share in the ruling. Despite the difference between five cities and ten cities, it shall be a tremendous honor for any Christian to reign with Christ.

The birth, the death, the resurrection, the ascension, and the life-giving element are all vital parts in the work of Christ; yet without His coming again and being King, Christians will only have hope in this life, thus being of all men most pitiable. The saints suffer today in this world, but they shall enjoy blessing in the future in heaven. However excellent heaven is, God does not grant it (but the kingdom) as compensation for the loss the saints incur in this world. The Lord Jesus must therefore return to *this* world. He was humiliated, despised, persecuted, and crucified in this world; therefore He must also be glorified in this world, not in some celestial realm elsewhere. Today Christians suffer with Christ. They suffer in the world, so they too will be glorified in this world. The coming again to be king is an inspiration not only to Christ but to His saints as well.

Furthermore, though the saints experience salvation of the spirit and the soul today, the redemption of their bodies still lies in the future (Rom. 8.23-25). Some believers have already died; they have not yet received their resurrection body. Some believers are still alive; they too have not obtained a transformed body. The spirit and the soul have been redeemed, but the body is waiting to be transformed by the Lord: "For indeed we that are in this tabernacle do groan, being burdened; not for that we would be unclothed, but that we would be clothed upon, that what is mortal may be swallowed up of life" (2 Cor. 5.4). We only know this—that at the time when the Lord shall come, the dead in Christ shall be resurrected and the living shall be transformed. How very essential the coming again of the Lord Jesus is. Even with the birth, death, resurrection, ascension, and life-giving aspects of Christ, salvation cannot be complete without His coming again because our bodies will not have yet been redeemed. As we observe the conditions of the world today, we are assured of the nearness of that day. Praise and thank God for that.

(7) The Seventh Day's Work Signifies the Lord Jesus in Eternity

On the seventh day, we saw no work performed by God (Gen. 2.1-3). There was neither word spoken nor work done. For the words had already been uttered and the works had all been accomplished. And thus there was neither need to speak nor to work. Nothing was now left to do except to indulge in divine satisfaction, to look back over the works of the Six Days and find it all good. The heart was satisfied because everything which needed to be done *had* been done. And with satisfaction now came rest. Satisfaction of the heart brought rest to the heart. The rest of the heart naturally carried with it the rest and peace of the whole being. As we have mentioned before, this day was different from the preceding six days because it had neither evening nor morning. The dark evening was forever past, and so was the morning. It now was eternal day.

The millennial kingdom is past and the eternal rest is at hand. Except for rest, there is nothing else. Such is to be the state of the new heaven and the new earth and New Jerusalem. The former darkness and misery have passed away. Even the best of the bygone days cannot be compared with this rest, even as the morning cannot be compared with the noonday. At that time, the work of the Lord Jesus is fully done: old things have forever passed away and eternity lies ahead. "Then cometh the end, when he [Christ] shall deliver up the kingdom to God, even the Father; when he shall have abolished all rule and all authority and power . . . that God may be all in all" (1 Cor. 15.24–28). Amen!

6 | Creation and Dispensation

In order to understand the Bible clearly we must study it according to its dispensational truth. God has a special way of treating people in a particular age or dispensation. And He has revealed to us that there are indeed dispensational distinctions in His word. If we read the Scriptures without a dispensational perspective we will find many contradictions which are hard to explain. Unbelievers take such contradictions as imperfectness on the part of the biblical writers in their concept of God—that their concept of God is gradually developed until it reaches fullness of understanding with the coming of the Lord Jesus. But this is the attitude and approach of the unbelieving who attempt to nullify the value of God's revelation. Naturally we refuse to accept such an approach. Yet we do recognize that there is a progressiveness of truth in the books of the Bible. What was considered as clear at the beginning of the Old Testament period is shown to be imperfect under the clearer light shed abroad in New Testament times. This is not because of men's different concepts of God, but because of the various degrees of God's revelation to men. Since God deals with men according to dispensation, He reveals himself gradually to them in accordance with what He requires of them in that particular dispensation.

We need to have a good understanding of the dispensations to be found in the Scriptures. Many regard the Bible as being divided timewise between the Old Testament and the New. Such a division obviously helps a great deal in the study of God's word; but it is not complete. Careful readers find the Bible to be a synthesis of seven dispensations. Such a seven-fold division is not an arbitrary one but will appear to be quite natural to anyone after a careful study is made of the Scriptures. Let us look briefly at each of these seven in turn.

The first of the seven dispensations is that of *innocency.* This was the time when Adam and Eve were in the Garden of Eden. The second dispensation to be found is that of *conscience,* which covers the period from the time that Adam's conscience had been awakened and he was driven out of Eden until the conclusion of the Flood. The third is that of *human government,* which extends from after the Flood to the dispersion of Babel. The fourth dispensation is one of *promise.* This begins with the call of Abraham and ends with the exodus of the children of Israel from Egypt. The fifth is that of *law,* commencing with the giving of the law at Mount Sinai and concluding with the cross of Calvary. The sixth dispensation is *grace,* which commences with the death of the Lord Jesus and the descent of the Holy Spirit and is to end with the rapture of the saints. The seventh and final one is that of the *kingdom,* which is to be ushered in at the second coming of Christ with the establishing of His millennial kingdom upon the earth and will conclude at the end of His thousand-year rule. After this millennium, the first heaven and the first earth will be consumed by fire and God shall create a new heaven and new earth. And eternity is then ushered in.

From the above analysis, we can readily see that the two most important dispensations in the Bible are those of law and grace. These two have occupied the longest periods of time and have been recorded the most in the Scriptures. During these various dispensations, we find that men's original state, God's covenants with them, their fall and God's judgment of them are all different. God deals differently with the people living in these various dispensations. Now if we are ignorant of these distinctions, then we will expect the people of one dispensation to keep the law of the other, thus causing much confusion as well as misunderstanding of God's word. These seven dispensations in the Bible deal primarily with the distinctive ways by which God treats men.

Yet the *overall* purpose of these seven dispensations is to show men how they *must depend on grace,* and not works, in order to be saved. Galatians 3 tells us that the purpose of God in giving promise to Abraham is that men may be saved by grace. Yet men neither confessed their sins nor acknowledged their weakness. They refused to believe that they could not be saved by works. In order therefore to show them their sins and their inability to do good, God added law after He had given promise to Abraham so as to cause them at last to know themselves. All the commandments and statutes in God's law were promulgated to expose the frailty and uncleanness within men. And thus they might be induced to receive grace.

According to human nature, no one likes grace. For all men reckon themselves good and able—that they have no sin and that they may be saved by good works. God must therefore cause men to truly know themselves before they will confess how utterly helpless they are. But once they confess themselves to be sinners, they will humble themselves to accept God's grace.

Now it took more than fifteen hundred years under the dispensation of law to prove to the world that there is none who can keep God's law and do good. And following the test of those fifteen centuries and more, God finally revealed His real purpose in the dispensation of grace, thereby showing men how they can be saved by believing in His grace. This grace was given to the world through the substitutionary death of the Lord Jesus for us sinners. Yet how sad that even today many people still do not acknowledge their sinfulness and are still trying to be saved by works. Such people should go back to the dispensation of law and be tested in that manner so as to enable them to know themselves.

This much we ought to say here about the

teaching of the seven dispensations. Now, though, we would like to point out how the story of the creation in Genesis 1 depicts the teaching of these seven dispensations found in the Bible.

Before we proceed, however, we want to comment on one particular verse in the Scriptures. We know that there are a thousand years in the seventh dispensation for it is to be the millennial kingdom. Revelation 20.4 explicitly mentions that this dispensation of the kingdom is in fact to be one thousand years. Many people are mistaken in their thinking to believe that this millennial kingdom is typified in the Creation story by the sabbath. Since this sabbath in such thinking would have to be a thousand years long, then according to 2 Peter 3.8 the preceding six days would have to be six thousand more years. They thus take the seven days of creation to be a type of the seven thousand years of world history. Their assumption is based on the passage in 2 Peter which says that "one day is with the Lord as a thousand years" (v.8). This is a mistake.

We should understand that the teaching of 2 Peter 3.8 is not that the Lord actually looks at one day as a thousand years; instead, it teaches the saints that time is nothing in God's sight. He is the eternal God, therefore time has absolutely no effect on Him. If we were to say that because one day is as a thousand years with the Lord the seven days of creation must therefore mean seven thousand years, how then are we to explain the concluding words of 2 Peter 3.8: ". . . and a thousand years [is] as one day"? For would not this demand that the thousand-year reign of Christ's kingdom be but one day in length? Yet that would be absurd!

Hence the real meaning here in 2 Peter 3 is that during the days of the longsuffering of God, He looks upon a thousand years as being but one day—that is to say, He views His own longsuffering as being short in duration. On the matter of delay, though, He deems one day to be a thousand years long; by which is meant that God regards the delay of even just one day as being a thousand years. All this speaks of the faithfulness of His promise and the immensity of His grace. And that is precisely what the succeeding verse in 2 Peter 3 bears out: "The Lord is not slack concerning his promise, as some count slackness; but is longsuffering to you-ward, not wishing that any should perish, but that all should come to repentance" (v.9).

Dispensation of Innocency

Let us now return to our theme. The words "In the beginning God created the heavens and the earth" in Genesis 1.1 speaks of the dispensation of innocency. What God created was perfect, beautiful and without blemish. In the dispensation of innocency, this was also true of mankind. But the heavens and the earth created by God did not remain long in this beautiful state. For the second verse tells us that "the earth [became] waste and void; and darkness was upon the face of the deep." The earth God created had changed. It received God's judgment and fell into desolation. It lost its former beauteous perfection.

Such can serve as a picture of man having to be driven out of the Garden of Eden because he had sinned and fallen. Instead of obeying God's order, Adam and Eve had followed the word of Satan. What they now received were the judgment and wrath of God. They lost the privilege of dwelling in the pleasant Garden of Eden. They were now naked, accursed, and cast out. Though they were given skins to wear, they had lost their original glory. Hereafter, they must sweat in labor for their living and suffer pain in childbearing. And thus is how the first dispensation of innocency began and ended.

Dispensation of Conscience

The work of the first day can appear as a type of the second dispensation—that of conscience—because this day's work resembles the state of things existing before the Flood. Although light had shone, it had not intervened or corrected any existing condition of the created things. Light merely exposed the ruin. Spiritually speaking, even though men have their conscience awakened to know good and evil, they do not have God's help to overcome the sin within them nor the sins they commit without. Apart from revealing that man is sinful, the conscience has no power to cause him to do good. Hence the work of conscience is like the light of God which shines into the sinner's heart and exposes the fact of his many defeats. But just as the light of the first day could render no help to the desolate world, so conscience can render no comfort to the sinful man.

Dispensation of Human Government

The work of the second day was to make heaven (it is "heavens" in Darby's translation of Gen. 1.8). It is not difficult to discover the meaning of "heavens" in Scripture: "the heavens do rule" (Dan. 4.26). Judging by its use in the Bible, the phrase "the heavens" mainly means authority and exalted position. Yet here in the Genesis story there were waters above the heavens. Water, by nature, is the most unstable thing in the world. Combining the meaning of waters with that of the heavens, we can readily perceive that in spite of authority there is much instability and weakness. This day's work is thus a type of the dispensation of human government. After the Flood the Lord gave to men the authority of government. Before the Flood and at the death of his brother Abel, Cain could say: "Am I my brother's keeper?" (Gen 4.9b) But after the Flood the commandment of God was this: "Whoso sheddeth man's blood, by man shall his blood be shed" (Gen. 9.6). This plainly speaks of human government, for now God had delivered to men the authority to execute the death penalty. Nevertheless, although there was now governmental authority, the one who received such authority was as unstable and weak as water. Noah was the one who received this command, yet not very long afterwards he got drunk and lay naked. This indicated his weakness. Even though God did not announce that this day's work was good, there is no doubt that His intention *was* good, since human government was established by God himself. Although

He could not bless it, He nonetheless uses it for men to receive a blessing.

Dispensation of Promise

The third day's work is a type of the dispensation of promise. On that day, the dry land was separated from the waters. According to the teaching of Daniel 7.2,3,17 and Revelation 17.15, we know that the waters refer to the Gentiles among the human race. Land, on the other hand, represents the Jewish nation. This distinction we can find frequently in the prophets. For each time a book of any prophet mentions "the land," such a phrase always points to the land of Judea. So, the land appearing out of waters typifies the Jews being separated from among the Gentiles. The dispensation of promise began with the call of Abram. His departure from Ur of Chaldea was like the land which came out of the waters. Israel as God's chosen people began with Abraham. His call to be separated from the Gentiles marked the commencement of the separation from the world of the children of Israel by God. The purpose in separating the land from the waters was in order for the land to bear fruits. This leads us to the second part of the third day's work.

Dispensation of Law

We have mentioned several times that the third day's work was divided into two parts: the first part called for the dividing of the dry land from the waters; and the second part was done to enable the earth to bear fruits. We have seen how the first part of the third day's work typifies the dispensation of promise. Now the second part of the third day's work is a type of the dispensation of law. God gave the law to the children of Israel that they might bear fruit. The law acted like a plow which could plough deep into the soil of the human heart that it might bring forth fruit. Hence the original intention of God in giving the law to the children of Israel was for them to produce fruit. No fruit could be produced in the Gentile waters, for God could not demand the nations to produce fruit to glorify Him. What God wished to pay attention to was the land. By the law He sowed seed as it were into the nation of Israel. And He was like the owner of the garden who from time to time sent His servants to the tenants to collect the fruit (see Matt. 21.33–41). We know how little fruit the children of Israel produced for God. Still, He used them to produce fruit, for "salvation is from the Jews" (John 4.22b). The Lord Jesus was "born under the law" (Gal. 4.4). Moreover, He had kept the entire law and produced the best fruit. He was the true Israelite. And as regards the whole body of the children of Israel, they will yet bear fruit in the millennial kingdom.

Dispensation of Grace

The work of the fourth day (Gen. 1.14–18) typifies that sixth dispensation which is that of grace. The heavenly bodies of light (the sun, moon, and stars) speak clearly of Christ and His church. Like the sun, Christ appears in the hearts of men through the power of the Holy Spirit that they may know His grace. In this dispensation, the church, like the moon in relation to the sun, is responsible to reflect the light of Christ. This age may be described as one long night. Christ (the sun) has ascended to heaven, and therefore the church (the moon) and the saints (the stars) are the only luminaries of this world. Let us remember that all enlightenment comes from heaven above. We as reflectors of that enlightenment must shine before the world. It means that we must show this world that we belong to another world. Just as Christ is not of this world, so we are not of this world either. We must let the world see that our living is heavenly in origin. Out of our joy and satisfaction in Christ we shine forth for Him. And this is how the church is to testify in this age of grace. Yet alas, how darkened is her light today! As the Bridegroom tarries, the light from her lamps unfortunately grows dim. If not from the torches of the overcoming virgins, where can the world ever obtain light? The light of the gospel is the characteristic of this dispensation of grace.

The Interlude

The fifth day's work (Gen. 1.20–23) is a type of the period of the Great Tribulation which follows the age of the church. We know that between the sixth dispensation (of grace) and the seventh dispensation (of the kingdom), there is a short period of time called the Great Tribulation. This will be a time of trials for the inhabitants of the earth.

In this fifth day's work, God again worked with the waters. During this period of the Creation story, the seas were rolling with waves. This is described in Psalm 93: "The floods have lifted up, O Jehovah, the floods have lifted up their voice; the floods lift up their waves"; but "above the voices of many waters, the mighty breakers of the sea, Jehovah on high is mighty" (vv.3,4).

This is the time when the world shall enter into trial. For it is to be "the hour of trial, that hour which is to come upon the *whole world,* to try them that dwell upon the earth" (Rev. 3.10). The waters, as we know, point to the Gentiles. During this period, the Gentiles will give themselves up to the lusts of their hearts and rebel against the Lord. They shall therefore be tested by Him: "Upon the earth distress of nations, in perplexity for the roaring of the sea and the billows; men fainting for fear, and for expectation of the things which are coming on the world" (Luke 21.25,26) —"for when God's judgments are in the earth, the inhabitants of the world learn righteousness" (Is. 26.9). So the waters swarmed with swarms of living creatures. During this period, God will prepare His earthly people for the day when they shall enjoy the blessing of the millennial kingdom.

While the inhabitants of the earth go through trial, God has also His work in the air. For in Genesis 1 God spoke not only of the living creatures in the waters, He spoke also of the fowls of the air. The spiritual significance of this is not hard to find. The

Bible tells us that while the inhabitants of the land, the Gentiles, are being tested under the judgment of God, the saints will be raptured by the Lord to the air: "Behold the birds of the heaven, that they sow not, neither do they reap, nor gather into barns; and your heavenly Father feedeth them. Are not ye of much more value than they?" (Matt. 6.26)—"Are not two sparrows sold for a penny? and not one of them shall fall on the ground without your Father: . . . Fear not therefore; ye are of more value than many sparrows" (Matt. 10.29,31). Does not all this speak of the Christians? Sparrows are living creatures in the air. Though they sometimes come down to earth, their home is in the air. For there they dwell and there they fly. It is ordained by God that the sparrows live above the earth in the air. The time is coming when "the Lord himself shall descend from heaven, with a shout, with the voice of the archangel, and with the trump of God: and the dead in Christ shall rise first; then we that are alive, that are left, shall together with them be caught up in the clouds, to meet the Lord in the air: and so shall we ever be with the Lord" (1 Thess. 4.16,17).

The Dispensation of the Kingdom

The sixth day's work of God in part was to create Adam and Eve and to appoint them to rule over the world (Gen. 1.26–28). This is a type of the seventh dispensation, that of the kingdom. The apostle Paul tells us in Romans that Adam is a figure of Christ who is to come (5.14). He also tells us in Ephesians that Eve (as alluded to in 5.31) is a figure of the church which will be presented to Christ holy and without blemish (Eph. 5.25-27,32). At that time Christ—in His capacity as "a son of man"—shall sit on the throne with His own (see Rev. 1.12; 3.21). This is God ruling through a man, and that man is Jesus Christ who has become man (1 Tim. 2.5).

In the work of this sixth day, we also saw that the earth brought forth many living creatures (Gen. 1.24,25). We have already mentioned the living creatures in the waters and the birds in the air. Now God's attention turns to the children of Israel who are represented by the land that emerged from the waters. During the millennial kingdom, not only will it be that those Gentiles who have passed through the tribulation shall become the nations, not only will it be that the saints shall reign with Christ, but also that the children of Israel shall once again be blessed by God and flourish according to all the promises which God had established in His covenant with Abraham, Isaac and Jacob as prophesied by the prophets: "In days to come shall Jacob take root; Israel shall blossom and bud; and they shall fill the face of the world with fruit" (Is. 27.6). Then shall God plant in the land again the people of Jezreel.*

Eternity

The rest on the seventh day is a type of the new

---

*Jezreel in the Bible is a symbolic name for Israel (e.g., cf. Hosea 1.4,11).—*Translator* heaven and the new earth in eternity upon the conclusion of the millennial kingdom. Seven dispensations have passed. What is now left is the sabbath. Hence the sabbath cannot be a figure of the millennial kingdom, since the latter will not yet be a time of rest. In the Creation story told of in Genesis, we find that on the sabbath or seventh day God rested from all His works (2.2). Spiritually speaking, God awaits the new heaven and the new earth before He can rest forever.

In the Genesis account of the Creation, there was no more day after the seventh day. For all works had been done, and God's heart desire had all been realized. So that God blessed this day as a day of rest. According to God's plan of restoration, symbolically speaking there are only seven days, after which there will be no more day. The work of redemption is finished and everything in God's eternal plan has been accomplished. There need be no more time to follow upon this perfect work of God. God simply appreciates and blesses what He has done. It is indeed true that He cannot rest before the time of the new heaven and the new earth because His work of redemption has not had its full effect. He will only rest when He sees all whom He has redeemed perfectly joined to the One Perfect Man, even Christ with all authority and blessing. This is eternity. Eternity is nothing less than resting in God's satisfaction and approval forever.

TITLES YOU
WILL WANT TO HAVE

By Watchman Nee

CD ROM – Complete works of Nee by CFP

Basic Lesson Series
Volume 1 – A Living Sacrifice
Volume 2 – The Good Confession
Volume 3 – Assembling Together
Volume 4- Not I, But Christ
Volume 5 – Do All to the Glory of God
Volume 6 – Love One Another

The Church and the Work
Volume 1 – Assembly Life
Volume 2 – Rethinking the Work
Volume 3 – Church Affairs
Revive Thy Work
The Word of the Cross
The Communion of the Holy Spirit
The Finest of the Wheat – Volume 1
The Finest of the Wheat – Volume 2
Take Heed
Worship God
Interpreting Matthew
The Character of God's Workman
Gleanings in the Fields of Boaz
The Spirit of the Gospel
The life That Wins
From Glory to Glory
The Spirit of Judgment
From Faith to Faith
Back to the Cross
The Lord My Portion
Aids to "Revelation"
Grace for Grace
The Better Covenant
A Balanced Christian Life
The Mystery of Creation

The Messenger of the Cross
Full of Grace and Truth – Volume 1
Full of Grace and Truth – Volume 2
The Spirit of Wisdom and Revelation
Whom Shall I Send?
The Testimony of God
The Salvation of the Soul
The King and the Kingdom of Heaven
The Body of Christ: A Reality
Let Us Pray
God's Plan and the Overcomers
The Glory of His Life
"Come, Lord Jesus"
Practical Issues of This Life
Gospel Dialogue
God's Work
Ye Search the Scriptures
The Prayer Ministry of the Church
Christ the Sum of All Spiritual Things
Spiritual Knowledge
The Latent Power of the Soul
The Ministry of God's Word
Spiritual Reality or Obsession
The Spiritual Man
The Release of The Spirit
Spiritual Authority

By Stephen Kaung

Discipled to Christ
The Splendor of His Ways
Seeing the Lord's End in Job
The Songs of Degrees
Meditations on Fifteen Psalms

ORDER FROM:

Christian Fellowship Publishers, Inc.
11515 Allecingie Parkway
Richmond, Virginia 23235